Cassius Dio

ANCIENTS IN ACTION

Boudicca, Marguerite Johnson
Callimachus, Richard Rawles
Catiline, Barbara Levick
Catullus, Amanda Hurley
Cleopatra, Susan Walker and Sally-Ann Ashton
Hadrian, James Morwood
Hannibal, Robert Garland
Homer, Jasper Griffin
Horace, Philip D. Hills
Lucretius, John Godwin
Marius, Federico Santangelo
Martial, Peter Howell
Ovid: Love Songs, Genevieve Lively
Ovid: Myth and Metamorphosis, Sarah Annes Brown
Pindar, Anne Pippin Burnett
Protagoras, Daniel Silvermintz
Sappho, Marguerite Johnson
Spartacus, Theresa Urbainszyk
Tacitus, Rhiannon Ash
Thucydides, P.J. Rhodes
Virgil, Jasper Griffin

Cassius Dio

Jesper Majbom Madsen

BLOOMSBURY ACADEMIC
LONDON • NEW YORK • OXFORD • NEW DELHI • SYDNEY

BLOOMSBURY ACADEMIC
Bloomsbury Publishing Plc
50 Bedford Square, London, WC1B 3DP, UK
1385 Broadway, New York, NY 10018, USA

BLOOMSBURY, BLOOMSBURY ACADEMIC and the Diana logo are
trademarks of Bloomsbury Publishing Plc

First published in Great Britain 2020

Copyright © Jesper Majbom Madsen, 2020

Jesper Majbom Madsen has asserted his right under the Copyright, Designs
and Patents Act, 1988, to be identified as Author of this work.

For legal purposes the Preface on pp. vi–viii constitute
an extension of this copyright page.

Cover design: Terry Woodley
Cover image © Heritage Auctions, HA.com

All rights reserved. No part of this publication may be reproduced or transmitted in any form or by any means, electronic or mechanical, including photocopying, recording, or any information storage or retrieval system, without prior permission in writing from the publishers.

Bloomsbury Publishing Plc does not have any control over, or responsibility for, any third-party websites referred to or in this book. All internet addresses given in this book were correct at the time of going to press. The author and publisher regret any inconvenience caused if addresses have changed or sites have ceased to exist, but can accept no responsibility for any such changes.

A catalogue record for this book is available from the British Library.

Library of Congress Cataloging-in-Publication Data
Names: Madsen, Jesper Majbom, author.
Title: Cassius Dio / Jesper Majbom Madsen.
Other titles: Ancients in action.
Description: London : Bloomsbury Academic, 2019. | Series: Ancients in action
Identifiers: LCCN 2019011544| ISBN 9781350033375 (pb) |
ISBN 9781350033368 (hpod)
Subjects: LCSH: Cassius Dio Cocceianus. Roman history. | Rome—History.
Classification: LCC DG206.C38 M34 2019 | DDC 937—dc23 LC record available
at https://lccn.loc.gov/2019011544

ISBN: HB: 978-1-3500-3336-8
      PB: 978-1-3500-3337-5
      ePDF: 978-1-3500-3338-2
      eBook: 978-1-3500-3339-9

Series: Ancients in Action

Typeset by RefineCatch Limited, Bungay, Suffolk

To find out more about our authors and books visit www.bloomsbury.com
and sign up for our newsletters.

Contents

Preface   vi

   Introduction   1
1   In Search of the Ideal Form of Government   25
2   Roman Narratives   57
3   Cassius Dio and His History of Rome   93

Conclusion   115
Notes   121
Bibliography   125
Index   131

Preface

My interest in the writings of Cassius Dio goes back many years. He first caught my attention in my undergraduate years of the 1990s, when I wrote an assignment on the civil war following the death of Julius Caesar. Dio followed me into my doctoral years and my studies on how the influence from Roman Rome rule was felt in Bithynia and Pontus, the province Dio was originally from. However, it was not until later that I developed a specific interest in Dio as an author. This happened on a summer's day in the Danish city of Kolding in 2010 when, over lunch, my doctoral supervisor Tønnes Bekker-Nielsen suggested that I made Dio my focus point in my tenure application at the University of Southern Denmark. It was the start of an exciting journey in the company of Dio, his text, my students in Odense and scholars from all over the world of classics and ancient history who share similar interests in the work of this third-century CE historian who has been repeatedly quoted but has not until recently had the attention his work really deserves.

With this book I hope to share my interests in Dio with others who work on historiography, specifically looking at an introduction to Dio's thoughts on Rome's political history. I hope to draw attention to the benefit of reading not only Dio but any ancient historian or commentator in full, which is the only way to fully appreciate the thoughts and agenda of the author. All too often Dio's work has been read in a selective manner, which has led scholars to believe that he did not have a real agenda when writing his eighty books of history other than to write as much of Rome's history as he could, from the foundation of the city to the moment he withdrew himself from public life in Rome in 229 CE.

I have benefitted from the help and inspiration of a number of people who have helped to improve this manuscript. In 2013, I taught a Master's course at the University of Southern Denmark, where I read all of what is left of Dio's eighty books. It was one of the most stimulating teaching experiences that I have ever had the privilege to be part of. Several good dissertations came out of this course, and I am grateful to say that they have been a strong inspiration to my thoughts on Dio's thinking, also in regards to this book. I am particularly grateful to Jakob Fløe, Mads Ortving Lindholmer and Christoffer Vassaux who continued their studies of Dio after they left university and with whom I have had the good fortune to meet again at conferences.

A number of my colleagues in classics and history in Denmark and abroad have contributed insightful thoughts and taken the time to consider and discuss my ideas at conferences or after a paper. In this respect, I am profoundly grateful to Carsten Hjort Lange who, although sometimes reluctantly, has shared a large part of my journey with Dio. We hosted a conference titled *Cassius Dio: Greek Intellectual and Roman Politician* together, published under the same title by Brill in 2016, and later organized an international network, Cassius Dio: Between History and Politics. A deep-felt thanks also goes to George Hinge, Adam Kemezis and Josiah Osgood who took the time to become part of the network's organizing committee. In the course of the two and a half years that the network lasted, I have enjoyed the expertise of Andrew Scott, Christopher Baron, Brandon Jones and Marianne Coudry, and I am looking forward to future projects with them.

I have had the pleasure of working on Dio during longer visits at various institutions. In this respect, I would like to thank Jason König and the School of Classics at the University of St Andrews; Greg Woolf and the Institute of Classical Studies in London; Alain Gowing, Department of Classics at the University of Washington; and Antonio Pistellato from the Ca' Foscari University of Venice. I would also like to thank Christopher Burden-Strevens for reading the entire manuscript and for his many useful comments, and Roger Rees for reading and improving the text and assisting with the adaption of the English translation of *Dio's Roman History*, first published by Earnest Cary between 1914 and 1927 in the Loeb Library series. Finally, I would like to offer my sincerest gratitude to Tønnes Bekker-Nielsen for the many stimulating conversations we have had over the past twenty years. This book is a product of the way of thinking he encourages day in, day out and of the inspiration he always is. I dedicate this book to him and to our long discussions, of which I hope there will be many more.

Odense, February 2019

Introduction

Cassius Dio was a man of action. He covered the longest period of Roman history that has come down to us by any ancient historian, and served as a much-trusted member of the imperial administration in some of the most turbulent years in the history of Rome. Dio was also a member of Rome's political elite for more than four decades. He entered the Senate sometime in the reign of Commodus (180–192 CE), and experienced, from his seat in the Colosseum, how the young emperor threatened the senators, such as when he showed them the severed head of an ostrich he had just killed in the arena and reminded them of what could soon be their fate should they fail to comply.[1] Dio later became Praetor in the reign of Pertinax (1 January to 28 March 193) for the year 194 and a man of greater importance when appointed to Septimius Severus' (193–211) *Consilium Principis*, after writing a pamphlet on how dreams and portents were predicting Severus' accession to the throne.

A link to the new emperor was now established, and Dio was later elected consul, maybe as a mark of gratitude on the part of the emperor. The dates for when Dio served as consul are unclear, and various dates between 205 and 211 have been suggested.[2] As a man from Bithynia, Dio was also the obvious choice as a member of Caracalla's (209–217) entourage when the young emperor travelled to western Asia Minor, where he visited Nicomedia, the capital of Bithynia. In 218, Macrinus (217–218) chose Dio as his curator for Pergamum and Smyrna, where he served until 222 before he was sent to govern Africa and Dalmatia by the emperor Elagabal (218–222), and later to Pannonia in the reign of Alexander Severus (222–235). As a reward for his service, Dio was honoured by a second consulship on his return in 228, serving with the emperor as his colleague.[3]

The second consulship was not the experience Dio had hoped for. As governor in Pannonia he was the commander of the armies in the province. Here, he tried to discipline the soldiers to a degree that caused the army to request that he be prosecuted. In Dio's version, the emperor did not listen to the complainant, and it was his attempt as governor to improve military discipline that earned him the second consulship (Dio 80[79].4.2–80[79]5.1). That Alexander may have listened more to the complaints than Dio wants us to believe, is suggested by the fact that the emperor asked Dio to leave Rome to serve as consul in his villa in Campania – because the emperor feared that the soldiers would harm him should he appear publicly as consul.[4]

As a participant in Roman politics from the late second century and a trusted member of the imperial administration, particularly in the 220s, Dio observed the political chaos after the death of Marcus Aurelius (161–180) from his seat in the Senate. His own experience as senator, as one of Rome's magistrates and as a trustee of several different emperors, determined how Dio perceived Roman politics as well as the history of Rome. As we shall see in the course of this book, Dio was, in many ways, well placed to witness, analyse and understand Roman political history as it developed, from the moment the city was founded to the late 220s when he left a troubled empire struggling to keep the peace both internally and at its borders.[5] In Dio's eyes, Rome's political system was facing an existential crisis. The senators were losing the privileged position that they had enjoyed for centuries, and responsibility for military administration was gradually shifting from the senators to members of the equestrian order. It was a change that had been under way for some time but it accelerated when Severus and Caracalla openly favoured the interests of their soldiers over any other groups in Roman society.

For good and bad, Dio's years in the Senate and imperial administration gave him the inside knowledge to draw on when analysing Roman political history in its *longue durée*. However, Dio had difficulty keeping his own first-hand experience out of his analysis. But unlike other ancient historians, who did not have the same personal experience of civil war, such as Appian and Tacitus, Dio offers a different interpretation of the city's political history; that interpretation is not only more personally engaged but is also more attentive to the vicious nature of war between citizens.

Coming in from Bithynia

If Dio was a special case as a historian, the path he followed to the centre of Roman politics was one he shared with many other young members of the elite. As a man of Greek origin from Bithynia in the north-western part of Asia Minor and a member of one of the most influential families in his home city, Dio had the right background and the right kind of forefathers to do well in Rome.

By the time he followed his father Cassius Apronianus to Rome and probably later to Cilicia, as part of Apronianus' staff, the political establishment in Rome was already acquainted with the Cassii from Nicaea. One of Dio's possible wealthy forefathers was Cassius Asclepiodotus, who had his property confiscated by Nero (54–68) because of ties to Barea Soranus (con. 52 CE), one of the conspirators against Nero. Asclepiodotus stood by his friend, received his punishment and was later restored by Galba (68 CE). Another ancestor, Cassius Philiscus, the son of Asclepiodotus, was a man of much renown in Nicaea, where an obelisk stood as the centrepiece of his family's grave monument. Philiscus was also a member of the Bithynian aristocracy, where he might have had a role to play in administration as a member of the provincial council or in the imperial cult as a priest or high priest in the provincial worship of the emperor.[6]

Another prominent man in first-century Nicaea was C. Cassius Chrestus. He acted as an agent for M. Plancius Varus, the governor of Bithynia, for whom he oversaw the restoration of the eastern gates, where a statue group of the Flavian emperors were looking down on travellers. From Chrestus' sarcophagus, found outside the gate in the opposite direction from Philiscus' obelisk, we know that Chrestus held several posts that were linked to the emperor. He was a *sebastophant*, whose task it was to carry images of the emperor in processions during festivals. He later became a priest – probably the high priest of the imperial cult on the provincial level – and served as ambassador, presumably also to the emperor.[7]

Since his grave lay in the opposite direction from Philiscus' obelisk, it may by that Chrestus belonged to a different branch of the Cassii in Nicaea, but there is really no way to be certain. However, it is beyond any doubt that Dio's father met the property qualification for election to the Senate and that, even if Asclepiodotus was not among his forefathers, he was from a family that was to be counted among the highest social elite in Bithynia.

When Dio and his father left for Rome some time in the reign of Marcus Aurelius, Nicaea was a city where most members of the local elite would have been Roman citizens. Like Chrestus, members of the local elite were for the most part keen to underline their loyalty to Rome and to the emperor. Up through the imperial period, Nicaea had competed with Nicomedia to be acknowledged either as the *first* city, the *metropolis*, mother city of the province, or to secure one of the provincial cults to the worship of the emperors. Judging from the epigraphic material from Nicaea, the city fits the picture of the rest of Asia Minor, where members of the political elite were eager to advertise their belonging to the community of Roman citizens across the empire, and made an effort to underline their membership of one or more Roman institutions: the administration of the imperial cult, provincial councils, the army, Roman politics or in imperial administration. The epigraphic material also unveils a widespread use of Roman names that testifies to the spread of Roman citizenship. Roman names, even of female members of families with no political opportunity of their own, were becoming an integral part of the local culture. There was little political momentum to be gained by giving Roman names to girls but it underlined to the rest of the city that the family was to be counted among the Roman citizens in the city or, in the case where they did not hold Roman rights, it still showed an affinity with Rome.

There is a scholarly tendency to understand identity in the Greek provinces as a matter of being Greek or Roman. Greeks are believed to have been more protective of their cultural origins than other ethnic groups within the empire were; and to have cherished their Greek cultural background more than other provincials. This has led to the conclusion that Greeks, who believed themselves to be culturally superior to every other people, were less likely to identify themselves as Romans, at least in the cultural sense of the word.[8] But this either/or approach is too simplistic to embrace fully the construction of identity.

Another way forward is to view identity as individual and as a composite of the groups and collectivities people were either part of or excluded from. A member of the political elite in Nicaea, Cassius Chrestus was a member of the civic elite in his home town, a Roman citizen, perhaps a priest in the imperial cult or in one of the other cults in the city, and someone who was proud of his connections to the Roman governor of Asia M. Plancius Varus, whom he called his friend and assisted with projects in the city. Chrestus was undeniably Greek. For all we know, he lived all or most of his life in Nicaea, and was no doubt well-rooted in his Greek cultural background. But he was also a proud Roman citizen and a part of the empire-wide collectivity of Roman citizens eager to advertise their roles and contributions in the upkeep of Roman power.[9]

Like Chrestus, Dio was a member of a number of quite different groups. He was a man of Nicaea, the city he chose to return to at the end of his life. He was Greek, and he pointed that out occasionally in his writing. He would have been schooled in much the same fashion as other boys from the wealthy families in any Greek province.[10] Like his peers, he would have studied Greek grammar, literature, rhetoric, geometry and perhaps music and, as he grew older, athletics. But Dio was Roman as well, and a member of the collectivity of Roman citizens in Nicaea, Bithynia and across the empire. He was a member of the Senate, which continued as a rather exclusive club even by the end of his life, to which only a small group of people could ever hope to gain access. He represented Rome when he travelled with Caracalla, when he served as a curator in Smyrna and Pergamum and when he governed Africa, Dalmatia and Pannonia as a highly-experienced member of the imperial administration. From his writing, it is clear that Dio was proud of his own career in Roman politics and administration, and of his father's.

That he saw himself as an established member of the elite in Rome is underlined from several references to the senators, when he talks about 'our' soldiers or when he states directly that Rome was his new home (Dio frg. 1.3 and 74.17.4–5). Dio was Greek, but he was also a Roman who was fully integrated into Rome's political establishment. Here he moved in the highest social circles: a status underlined by the appointments to Dalmatia and Pannonia, two key provinces to the emperor. Dio also joined the intellectual circle organized by Julia Domna, the wife of Septimius Severus, and he was later appointed to a second consulship with Alexander Severus as his colleague. However, he was also a dedicated historian who devoted more than twenty years of his life to writing a history of Rome that was inspired by Thucydides' Greek realism as well as Roman annalistic traditions.

Whether Dio's ties to his Greek background were more important to him than his Roman citizenship, the seat he held in the Senate, his belonging to the circle of trusted magistrates or his work as a historian would depend on the context. More important to how we are to understand Dio are the many different aspects of his life and the number of different groups and memberships he took part in, which together determined how he saw himself and how he was seen by his peers, the armies he commanded and the provincials he governed.

In the middle of the second century, when Dio and his father arrived in Rome, members of the Greek urban elite were already a well-integrated part of Roman politics and intellectual life. The number of Greek senators had steadily increased so that by the middle of the second century, half of the non-Italian members were from one of the Greek provinces.[11]

Emperors such as Hadrian (117–138) and Marcus Aurelius, both praised by Greek intellectuals, showed a profound interest in and respect for Greek culture, art and architecture. Both studied Greek philosophy and Aurelius wrote a book on his own thoughts, which was inspired by stoic thinking. For a long time, emperors had included learned Greeks among their advisors, and used Greeks as secretaries, tutors and intellectual entertainment. Members of the Greek intellectual elite in the second and third century, men such as Aristides and Philostratus, were also well aware that the Greeks and their culture were an established and, in their eyes, indispensable part of the empire's cultural and intellectual life. They continued to promote the superiority of Greek civilization and encouraged their fellow Greeks to seize the moment and embrace what the empire had to offer, including memberships of the different Roman institutions of power such as the citizenship and a place in the empire's social and political elite.

Son of a senator

As the son of a senator, a consul and governor of Cilicia and Dalmatia, Dio did not have to work his way up the social ladder in the same way as the *homines novi*, the new men, who were the first in their families to earn a seat in the Senate. Dio probably served his ten years in the Roman cavalry or under the leadership of his father in the army or in Cilicia, but he did not have to follow the much longer route as an officer in the army, like his father had done before entering the Senate from the officers' rank. Instead, he was ready to start on his first office as *quaestor*, an administrative post with financial responsibilities at Rome or in the provinces, sometime in the age of Commodus. Later he would have become *Aedile* with responsibility for games, temples, water supplies and the supervision of the marketplace.

Based on Dio's own words, which in effect is all we have, there is no reason to assume that he would have felt anything other than at home in Rome and as a natural member of the city's elite establishment. By the mid-second century CE, Rome had been one of the most important cultural centres in the empire for more than a century. Many of the empire's most talented men of letters, artists, architects and philosophers had come to Rome from all over the empire to get their share of the city's wealth. Dio was therefore well placed to continue his Greek education but also to pursue other interests such as in Roman history, Latin and Latin literature, which he must have read enthusiastically in order to write a history as long and as detailed as his. Also, judging from his energetic speech-writing and how speeches *per se* carried enormous importance as a forum, where Dio offers his own opinion or demonstrates a person's character, he would, in all likelihood, have studied the *Institutio Oratoria* of Quintilian. He would also have read some of Cicero's many speeches and a variety of other Roman orators from the Republic, which he used as a source of inspiration when composing speeches by himself to add an extra layer to the narrative.

Dio's history of Rome

Even if it is not always acknowledged as such, Dio's *Roman History* is one of the most important sources for the history of Rome. The first twenty-four books, from the foundation of Rome to the death of Tiberius Gracchus, are often neglected. However, even if in a fragmentary state, these books offer a remarkably detailed and coherent analysis of Roman politics, stressing that the early and middle republic were considerably less free from internal political instability than ancient historians tend to acknowledge. With a continuous focus on strife between the social layers and in between members of the political elite, Dio describes how force and politically-motivated violence always played an integral part in Roman politics, not just in the Regal Period, but throughout the Republic.[12]

Books 36–61 cover the years from the 70s when Pompey the Great entered the Senate and the consular office, to the beginning of the reign of Claudius (41–54). Apart from book 61, these books contain Dio's own text, whereas the last thirty books from 61 to 80 have come down to us in epitome, the excerpts that the Byzantine scholar Xiphilinus wrote in the latter half of the eleventh century. In books 36–61, Dio offers his readers an unparalleled narrative of Roman politics from the Late Republic to the moment that the principate was finally settling in as a new form of constitution after some turbulent years in the reign of Caligula (37–41).

In the course of these books, Dio discusses the fall of the Republic and provides his own analysis of the political crisis that brought Republican Rome to its fall, including how strong political protagonists such as Cornelius Sulla, Gaius Marius, Pompey, Caesar and Octavian came to power and why they drew fellow Romans and the entire empire from one civil war to the next.

The thirty books in the excerpts of Xiphilinus offer an abbreviated version of Dio's account from the reign of Claudius to the moment he withdrew from the political scene in Rome. As we shall see in Chapter 2, short as some of the excerpts are, one recognizes the outline of a well-organized argument that demonstrates what defined both the qualified and the incompetent ruler. Even when abbreviated by others, Dio's work remains the most important written source for the history of the second century CE – the age of the adoptive emperors – and for the early decades of the third century when Dio was politically active in Rome. That a large part of the original text has come down to us in excerpts presents students of Dio with a number of challenges. If in order to condense the text, Xiphilinus took out paragraphs rather than rewrote the text in an abbreviated form, nonetheless he interfered with the original version by changing the focus of Dio's narrative. It has been argued recently that one of Xiphilinus' principal interests was the character of emperors rather than the political history of Rome.[13] Of course, this has implications when the excerpts are used to establish what Dio thought of certain emperors or how he describes particular situations or episodes, but they remain the most reliable surviving account for the second and early third centuries. For better or worse, Dio offers a highly engaged and personalized account of Rome's political history, both of earlier periods and of his own lifetime.

Even if an ancient book compares to a modern chapter, writing eighty books on more than 1,000 years of history was still an ambitious task at a time when texts were produced by hand and were hard to come by. Editing text was possible but must have been a slow process. Larger changes might require considerable reproduction of existing passages, and new copies had to be produced one at a time. Access to texts on history and philosophy, and collections of letters or other written material were difficult to find, even for members of the intellectual elite. Rome and other major cities such as Athens, Alexandria, Smyrna, Ephesus and Antioch had well-equipped libraries but writers could not hope these libraries would have all the books they needed – even if they worked in some of the better-stocked libraries. Ancient writers faced challenges similar to those confronting modern historians and classicists, when a lot of ancient texts are lost in part or whole. Also, ancient writers of history would have been forced to rely on their memory of what they had once read or heard about, either at a reading or from a discussion with others with historic interests.

Although access to copies of certain works of history was a challenge that faced all ancient writers, it was even more so to authors such as Dio who wanted to write the history of longer timespans. To write eighty books was no doubt an ambitious task. Dio claimed it took him more than twenty years from when he began collecting material to the moment he finished writing in the late 220s or early 230s (Dio 72.23). However, it was not sufficient space to provide a consistently detailed and systematic account of the entire span of these years, or to give thorough characterizations even of the main protagonists in the narrative.

As a consequence, individuals essential to the account are often introduced into the narrative abruptly and without background information. For example, certain episodes, such as the Catiline conspiracy and Cicero's role in it, are given a superficial coverage in book 38. Key episodes lack attention to detail, and sometimes Dio is guilty of sloppy handling of facts and a style of writing where events are grouped together out of convenience. This has led scholars to conclude that Dio did not possess the same quality as his more renowned fellow historians, such as Livy, Sallust and Tacitus or Thucydides.

In the late nineteenth century and first half of the twentieth century, Dio was seen as a copyist with few ideas of his own, who reproduced in his own words the thoughts and narratives of earlier and better historians, using only one source at a time. This unfavourable view was finally modified in the middle of the 1960s by Fergus Millar. Although Millar's re-evaluation was recognized as a milestone in scholarship, the *Roman History* was still seen (also by Millar) as ill-planned and too big for Dio to offer his readers thorough accounts and analysis of the main events in Roman history. Instead, Millar saw Dio as someone who worked without a framework for interpretation of the events he narrates, and who had no aim other than to cover as much of Rome's history as possible: as someone who compiled information with little or no ambition to offer substantial political or historical analysis.[14]

Today it is widely acknowledged that Dio had no agenda when writing the history of Rome other than simply composing the text and covering as much of Rome's history as possible. It is now the consensus that he was heavily influenced by his own contemporary years and the turbulent times from the death of the emperor Marcus Aurelius to the moment when Dio left Roman politics. Of course, every historian is influenced by his or her own time and understands and interprets the past through the lens of the present. But some modern scholars see Dio as too caught up in his own age and its political chaos, civil war and violence to write about the past in its own right. This school of thought holds that Dio used at least part of what he wrote about earlier periods to encourage changes to the present political situation, including how the emperors were to rule or what the political establishment in Rome should be able to expect from the monarch. This, some scholars have argued, has led to reconstructions of the past where Dio writes flawed accounts, for instance on the reign of Augustus, which are more convincingly seen as comments on the rule of Septimius Severus.[15]

This, of course, would undermine Dio as a source for any period other than his own, but as we shall see in the following chapters, Dio offers considerably more than criticism of emperors and their way of governing in his own contemporary years. Similarly, the purpose of writing Rome's history from its origin up until the last years of Dio's life, was more ambitious than a desire to define what would be good governmental practices.

In recent decades, scholars have paid more attention to the many layers in the *Roman History* and to the different agendas that Dio worked from. Dio may well have hoped to immortalize himself, which he managed to do probably beyond his wildest expectations, and to add his name to the list of renowned historians. But when reading what has come down to us in Dio's own words and in the extracts, it becomes clear that the author followed several leads. One of the threads that runs through the narrative is the attempt to demonstrate how the city of Rome became a world power, much in the same fashion as the second-century BCE historian, Polybius from Greece. Another line of enquiry addresses why the various shifts in Roman politics occurred in the way they did; a third concentrates on the constitutional changes Rome experienced and on the political crises, instability and successes that changed the city's history.

Dio focuses on the troubled emperors of his own time and on the political turbulence that followed imperial assassinations, civil wars and prosecutions of members of Rome's senatorial elite. But as we shall see in the course of this book, Dio also wrote about Republican Rome: the functions, strengths and failings of Rome's institutions; the political elite and the ambition that brought the Republican form of constitution to dissolution.

Another key issue for Dio, as we shall see in the course of this book, was to prove that monarchy was indeed without any doubt the only reliable form of constitution, and to show that any other form of government, where the decision-making process rested on popular vote, was destined to fail. In Dio's mind, the competition between members of the political elite in the Republic led to disputes, strife and civil war, and would do the same again if a democratic form of government was reintroduced. Another aim was to offer his point of view on how to organize the best form of monarchical rule. With examples of good and inadequate forms of government, and a coverage of the rule of both capable and inadequate emperors, Dio not only seeks to define a competent emperor but also to demonstrate how Rome was governed differently at different times, from the accession of Augustus to the reign of Alexander Severus. It is true that much of this discussion ties into questions that were highly relevant at the time Dio lived in Rome but, as I hope to show, the intention behind writing Rome's history in its entirety was more than an ambition to add his own thoughts to contemporary debate about good governmental practice, or to offer the emperors of his own day examples of good governmental practices.

Two aspects point in this direction. One is from the dialogue between Augustus' friends and advisors Agrippa and Maecenas, where Maecenas offers his advice on how Augustus should acquire absolute power and leave the Senate with the role of his advisory body without any political initiative of their own (Dio 52.14–40). If Dio's history was meant largely as a contribution to a current debate about government and what defined the good and unfit emperor, it is inexplicable why he should suggest a form of government that would allow emperors such as Caracalla (one of the emperors Dio despised the most) unrestricted power, including full control over the army, the right to appoint magistrates and officers, and the undivided responsibility for writing and implementing new laws.

Another element that suggests Dio was not simply caught up in his own day and age is how monarchical rule is not questioned. Not once in the course of the narrative does Dio entertain the idea that another form of constitution could be the solution to the problem of the incapable emperors who dominated his contemporary Rome. One would think that the performance of Commodus, Didius Julianus

(193), Caracalla, Macrinus and Elagabal would give him reason to reconsider his thoughts on monarchy. Dio questions the monarch but never the monarchy.

One purpose of this book is to offer an introduction to the historian and politician Cassius Dio, how he worked and wrote his history of Rome. The aim is to show the many different agendas Dio had, and to demonstrate that the motives he had were politicized, such as when he shaped a narrative so that the failings of what he calls 'democracy', Rome's republican constitution, are evident to his reader. Another aim is to make the case that Dio is a useful and capable historian whose analysis of Rome's political history has much to offer, even if the information or accounts of certain events, facts and motives of those involved are not always accurate. The question in the following is therefore not whether we can rely on Dio, but how he is best used as evidence in our attempt to understand Ancient Rome.

Having criticized Dio's many shortcomings, the same scholars still tend to use his books to reconstruct the history of Late Republican Rome, the age of Augustus and the imperial period, where he is the key literary source for the second and third centuries.[16] Other scholars have criticized the level of information Dio offers, the depth of his analysis or that he misses out some of the bigger challenges Rome faced in his own lifetime: Christianity and the pressure from Germanic and Persian tribes on the borders.[17]

Few have focused on what Dio does well and how he is best used as a source for different periods, specific episodes and the different political institutions that Rome operated, or for the acts and motives of men such as Caesar, Cicero and Octavian. Therefore, one of the questions to be discussed in the course of the following chapters is not only how to use Dio's text and the thoughts he offers on Roman politics, but also what it says about him as historian: the choices he made, the themes and episodes he focuses on, his biases and pre-dispositions.

To fully grasp the message and the underlying agenda that monarchical rule was the only constitutional option available to the Romans, Dio's narrative, or the large part that survives or may be reconstructed from the excerpts, has to be read in its entirety. When read together, it becomes clear that Dio built his account on a number of themes: how power corrupts, that people always strive for glory and success, and that the prestige to be earned from big political and military achievements always sparked a competition between members of the elite, which in the end led to political instability. As we shall see in the following chapters, greed, the urge for glory and supreme rule were not just phenomena that applied in the age of Republican Rome. They were an integral part of human nature and therefore some of that continued as a threat to political stability in the age of the empire.

Dio may be superficial and misleading at times, but as we shall see, he offers an in-depth analysis of the flaws and failings of the political system of Republican Rome, and in what way a monarchical form of government would provide a better alternative. He doesn't only focus on the 100 years from the violent death of the people's tribune Tiberius Gracchus in 133 BCE to the introduction of monarchical rule when Octavian won the civil wars against Antony in the year 30 BCE. He also offers a carefully-planned analysis of Roman politics in the entire age of the Republic. Here he is able to show how greed, envy and the struggle for power were well-established features in Roman politics throughout the history of the Republic and into the imperial period. In the same way, the *longue durée* of Dio's narrative enables him to compare the acts of leading Roman politicians in the earlier and middle republic with those of men such as Pompey, Caesar and Antony, to show how Roman politics developed over the course of centuries but also how in the early and middle Republic there were men of great renown with eyes for what was in the best interests of the state. Similarly, he shows that some of the same problems that threatened stability in Republican Rome continued into the Imperial age and showed their destabilizing potential from time to time. This was a reminder that the chaos of civil war could come back if the form of monarchical rule he promoted was not upheld.

Dio's analysis of Republican Rome has largely been forgotten, and his text is often used as a source of information to fill in gaps when no other evidence is available. But when he follows Roman politics from the fall of the kings in the late sixth century to the introduction of monarchical rule in the early 20s BCE, or when he gives specific examples to prove how greed, envy and ambition undermined Republican Rome, he offers a theoretical framework that explains why the Romans behaved in the way they did. As we shall see in Chapter 2, Dio's books are arguably the most detailed and consistent ancient analysis of the politics of Republican Rome.

Read in full, Dio's study of Imperial Rome and monarchical rule has more to offer than is traditionally acknowledged. In the course of the thirty books from book 51 to book 80, Dio provides a narrative of how Augustus shaped the monarchical constitution that was still functioning in the early third century, just as he provides his readers with a detailed account of how Augustus organized Roman politics and what he did to shape the political system that lasted for several centuries. The Agrippa–Maecenas dialogue in book 52 provides a theoretical discussion of how best to establish a functional monarchy that would not turn into a tyrannical form of government. What makes Dio particularly interesting is how he delivers a coherent account of what constituted both good and insufficient monarchical rule, when it was practised and how it was maintained.

Dio's bias was influenced by the ideals in senatorial Rome about how the capable emperors were those who asked the Senate for advice and made it their priority to honour the members of the senatorial order. However, Dio is able to step outside of general opinion when he offers a more nuanced portrait of an emperor such as Hadrian who was criticized for killing senators and other men of excellence, either to secure power or out of envy of their talents. In the portrait of Hadrian that Xiphilinus has left us, Dio emphasizes the emperor's ability to enforce discipline in the army, and how Hadrian moved away from his predecessor's expansionists strategies. Trajan (98–117) is another emperor of whom Dio offers a balanced portrait: he comes across not only as someone able to establish a harmonious relationship with the Senate, but also as someone who fought unnecessary wars, particularly in the East, out of a desire for glory and prestige (Dio 68.17.1).

Dio offers a very personal version of Imperial Rome: its emperors, their highs and lows, and the crisis Rome faced both in and before his own lifetime. In the course of his books, readers are introduced to a series of constitutional reflections on how to shape a more stable form of monarchy than the form of rule offered by most emperors, including all of Dio's contemporary emperors, except Marcus Aurelius and Pertinax. These thoughts are more ambitious than an attempt to strengthen the role of his peers or save what was left of the political privileges they had enjoyed up until the age of the Severan dynasty. Instead, with his *Roman History* Dio made an attempt to encourage real political changes both to the constitution and to the mindset of the political elite in Rome and at the imperial court.

Dio's Rome

The Rome in which Dio lived most of his life was marked by continuous instability, a strained relationship between the court and the Senate, and a political climate where most emperors died violent deaths after a brief rule. The army and the emperors' guard, the Praetorians, gradually gained more influence from the emperors who channelled ever larger funds towards the armed forces at a time when the throne was for sale to the highest bidder. From the death of Commodus onwards, the army and Praetorians chose the next emperor in a more transparent manner.

The Praetorians killed Emperor Pertinax three months after they had approved him; they also proclaimed Didius Julianus after he had won the empire in what Dio describes as an auction offering the Praetorians more than 20,000 sesterces each (Dio 74[73].11–12). It was also the army that killed Caracalla, something Dio was less troubled about, but it meant that Macrinus, the emperor's Praetorian prefect, assumed the throne as the first equestrian emperor ever to have ruled Rome, which was a development that our historian was less happy about (Dio 79[80].6–7).

From his coverage of his own time in Roman politics, it appears that Dio felt threatened by an army more visible in the streets of Rome and by the instability caused by the direct involvement of soldiers in the decisions about who was to become emperor – and for how long. The fear Dio felt from the emperors whose powers rested on the Praetorians' goodwill alone is clearly expressed in the case of Didius Julianus. Dio felt particularly exposed as one of the senators who had favoured Pertinax and because as an advocate he had pointed at the many crimes committed by the new emperor. Julianus' first speech as emperor in the Senate is covered by Dio, who describes how large numbers of Praetorians were posted both outside the Senate house and in the room where the meeting was held.

Another of Dio's concerns was the new round of civil war initiated when Septimius Severus fought first G. Pescennius Niger (193–194) and later D. Septimius Albinus (197) to win supreme power. Thousands of Roman soldiers died in the course of the two wars, and people in the provinces suffered considerably when the armies met on battlefields in their vicinity or when cities were forced to choose sides, decisions that could turn out to be catastrophic if the other party proved stronger. This happened to Dio's home region when Severus' army raided the city of Byzantium and as Nicaea lost its honorific titles as a punishment for having supported Niger.

One of the consequences of Severus' victory in the wars against Niger and Albinus was the return of dynastic rule, where the next emperor in line was the son or male relative of his predecessor and was chosen for dynastic reasons alone. As we shall see in Chapter 1, family succession and the reign of unequipped emperors represented a threat to monarchical rule and would, in Dio's view, best be avoided. Just as Dio shows how a 'democratic' form of government was unequipped to rule any state, but particularly one as powerful as Rome, he is also keen to demonstrate that dynastic succession was too unpredictable, since the next emperor in line would be elected not because he had the right qualities to rule or an interest in the task but because he happened to be his predecessor's son or male relative.

No doubt, the political chaos and threats from the civil wars Dio experienced first-hand had an impact on how he understood Roman politics. Therefore, his thoughts on what constitutes an ideal form of government tie in with his own experiences of the emperors of his day, just as his thoughts on civil war in Late Republican Rome were shaped by the uneasy times following the wars between Severus, Niger and Albinus, and the hostile relationship between Severus and at least part of the Senate following the last of the two wars.

Scholars are therefore right to point out that Dio was influenced by his own time. That applies to every historian who at any point in time understands the past through the lens of his or her own time. But the claim that Dio's dependency on his own contemporary years meant that he was too caught up in his own time to fully grasp, or at least convey balanced accounts of earlier periods, would be a hard critique of any historian and one that I hope to show is far from justified. His coverage might be superficial at times but at other times it is highly sophisticated, such as when he discusses Caesar's character or when he tries to convey to his reader that the civil war following the death of the dictator was not only justifiable but a necessary evil to introduce monarchical rule.

Furthermore, there is also a tendency to overlook the fact that Dio offers his own thoughts on how Roman decision-makers were to organize a form of monarchical rule that would ensure the political stability and prosperity that Romans had been longing for since the fall of Carthage in 146 BCE. What is often overlooked is how Dio's narrative offers a number of examples to show that some emperors managed to provide a stable form of government, and how he seems to have held the need for monarchical rule higher than the stress caused by inadequate emperors. If Dio had been unable to disregard the political instability of his own time, it is odd he would recommend a form of government that offered almost unrestricted powers to the emperor, leaving the members of the Senate as his loyal advisors.

Dio was a man of his time committed to what would have been a current debate on the best form of government. His eighty books on Rome's political history are surely a contribution to that debate, but what I also hope to show over the course of the book is that Dio offers a bigger picture, providing his readers with explanations for Rome's successes and failings, and solutions to the many different challenges that the city, its elite and the empire continuously had to face.

Chapter 1 is devoted to the agenda behind Dio's writing and to his thoughts about what constituted the ideal form of government and why, in his eyes, a monarchical form of government was the only way to ensure sufficient political stability and prosperity. Two questions stand at the centre of the discussion. What, in Dio's mind, constituted the right form of monarchy, and how were the emperors to discharge what was essentially unrestricted powers without falling into the trap of despotism? The second question orbits around the paradox: why does Dio argue in favour of a form of monarchical constitution where the emperors were to have essentially unlimited power at a time when most emperors in his lifetime were less than keen to uphold the illusion that the senators were valued partners in government?

In Chapter 2 we turn to how Dio shaped a narrative that demonstrates why democratic rule is incapable of providing political stability. In Dio's eyes, the notorious lack of modesty would always encourage a political culture where members of the elite would have to compete for the power and glory obtainable from the prestigious political and military posts. The second part of the chapter focuses on how Dio, in the course of his narrative, demonstrates that Augustus managed to organize a stable form of monarchical rule and how later emperors managed to succeed or fail as monarchs.

In Chapter 3, we turn to the question of how to use Dio as a source for Roman history. The chapter opens with a discussion of what kind of impact Dio had on other ancient writers. The second part of the chapter touches upon what Dio does well: the historical and political analysis he offers on the different periods in Roman history, his coherent argument about why Roman politics evolved in the way it did, and his careful recommendations about how to organize a political culture that would provide stability and peace.

As we shall see in the course of the book, one of his shortcomings ties into his scepticism towards democratic or republican ways of governing, which tempts Dio to overstate his critique of Rome's political elite. This is particularly evident in his narrative of Late Republican Rome, where essentially every member of the political elite was in politics to fulfil their own dreams and aspirations. Another of Dio's failings is his hatred of the Severan emperors, not least Septimius Severus who introduced the new age of dynastic succession. Dio paints a picture of the Severans, where he withholds vital information that would have offered a more balanced account of the decision they made at crucial moments. One such incident is when Dio fails to mention that the members of the Senate were encouraging Albinus's aspirations to become the next emperor. The information is offered by Herodian, Dio's younger contemporary historian, and would help to explain why the relationship between Severus and the Senate suddenly changed from promising and balanced to hostile and mean.

As we shall see in Chapter 3, Dio is also a historian who offers accounts of specific situations without which we would have had very little knowledge. This is the case with his coverage of what took place in the Italian city Perusia (modern Perugia) where, in the winter of 40 during the civil wars, Octavian forced the city to surrender. Here Dio's version of the events, in which Octavian is said to have slaughtered hundreds of Roman nobles in what seems to have been a kind of human sacrifice, might be the most reliable account of what comes across as a quite unbelievable story to begin with. Another example is from the reign of the emperor Tiberius (14–37), where Dio's account offers a solid analysis of how the emperor brought his Praetorian prefect Sejanus to a fall. It is time to turn towards the framework on which Dio based his Roman history: the urge to explain to his readers why monarchy was a superior form of government and was the only way to rule Rome in a stable and prosperous fashion. We open with how Dio was inspired by the realism in the writing of his great Greek predecessor, the historian Thucydides.

1

In Search of the Ideal Form of Government

One of the key perspectives in Dio's approach to Roman history, or history more generally, is that man, or human nature more broadly, is characterized by an inevitable urge to supersede other individuals in the group that he, or she, belongs to. This kind of realism goes back to the Greek historian Thucydides, who thought greed and hatred the two most important factors why people in the same communities fought and killed each other (Thuc. 3.83–85).[1] When Dio looked around his contemporary Rome, or when he took a moment to reflect on human behaviour in the late second and early third centuries CE, there were plenty of examples to confirm that fear, greed and the competition to ensure supreme power were still integral parts of political culture in the provinces and in Rome itself. One example offered by Dio is how the emperor Commodus suppressed and terrorized the Senate, the council of ex magistrates, because he dreaded the more experienced senators, or he took pleasure in their fear of him, or because he did not care to take their advice into consideration (Dio 73[72].15). Pertinax, the only emperor that Dio describes in largely positive terms, was murdered, as we saw in the Introduction, by the Praetorians when he tried to be firm with the soldiers who then moved on to accept Didius Julianus offer as it proved to be the highest bid for the throne (Dio 74[73].10).

When Niger was indecisive about a move from Syria back to Rome, Septimius Severus took advantage and destabilized Rome by his urge to win power for himself. New rounds of civil wars were fought first against Niger and then against Albinus, in an attempt to win supreme power, wars in which thousands of Roman soldiers lost their lives.[2] A new family dynasty, the first since the Flavians in the last decades of the first century CE, saw the light of day, even after Severus was almost killed by Caracalla when the two campaigned in Britannia and therefore after the emperor knew the true nature of his oldest son (Dio 77.[76]14). To Dio, Severus' quest for glory and the reputation of the family proved more important than the interests and security of the people in Rome and across the empire.

Therefore, Dio had no problem recognizing how immodesty, unfettered ambition and lust for power continued to be key factors in Roman politics from the foundation of the city to the 220s. Considering Dio's own experience of Roman politics, one obvious question is why he kept favouring a monarchical form of government at a time when one inadequate and despotic emperor followed another, and why he made it his most important message to convince the reader that a democratic form of constitution offered no alternative to monarchical rule. As we saw in the Introduction, like many other ancient commentators, Dio thought democracy was the source of untamed political ambition of members of the elite in the Senate, uncertainty, chaos, violent behaviour and eventually wars between citizens. Dio never once seems to question monarchy as the superior form of constitution, not even when he covers what he saw as the most unpredictable and tyrannical emperors: men such as Caligula, Commodus and Caracalla who were young and inexperienced at the time of their accession.

One answer is that Dio could not think of any real alternative to the form of constitution he describes as monarchy: one-man rule where the emperor had the responsibility for enacting new laws and making every political and military decision by himself, but not until he had listened carefully to the advice offered by his peers – that is the members of the Senate. The only other form of constitution available, in Dio's understanding, would be a Greek form of direct democracy, where each vote counted the same. This differed from how the voting was carried out in Rome's most influential assembly, the *comitia centuriata*, where the city's most important magistrates were elected. Here, since the early Republic, the people of Rome had voted according to their property qualification, in a system that left the underprivileged citizens without much influence on the election of the most prestigious magistracies.

In the other assembly, the *comitia tributa*, every vote counted the same. Votes were cast in tribes, which counted members of the entire citizen body and elected the lowest magistrates. From 287 BCE, proposals from the people's tribunes (the protectors of the commoners) that passed in the assembly counted as law, and the assembly turned into the most important legislative institution. But even if Dio has Agrippa promoting democracy in its Greek form in the dialogue between him and Maecenas, Octavian's close friends, the historian makes it abundantly clear in his own voice that democracy will fail, as the people grow gradually more self-confident and demanding of political influence and material goods (Dio 52.9.1–2 and 44.2.3).

As we shall see in the course of this chapter, another reason why Dio questions the stability of a democratic constitution is that he seems more concerned about free and open competition, where every member of the political elite was free to pursue their own ambition in a zero-sum game, and the success of someone would mean the failings of others. This competition for power and prestige, combined with a lack of modesty, had all the ingredients to promote a political culture where the privileged few were driven by fear and envy that they themselves would be superseded by their more successful peers, or not be powerful enough to keep others from fulfilling their aspiration for power.

It is true that personal ambitions, greed and desire to become Rome's next supreme ruler were an integral part of Imperial Rome, as

Dio knew only too well from a long career in Roman politics. However, as we shall see, in Dio's view a monarchical form of constitution would limit the competition between ambitious members of the elite, as military commands were no longer decided by public vote. Instead, it was the emperors who chose commanders and effectively the most important magistrates. Members of the political elite continued to compete with each other but now had to impress the emperor, instead of the public. From the reign of Augustus, commanders were no longer able to celebrate their military achievements under their own name, just as future appointments and opportunities to perform depended on whether the emperor chose to grant that individual another post.

In the way Dio sees it, the incentive to impress the voters was therefore a thing of the past and, essentially, the emperor's concern. When from time to time Roman generals fought to become the next emperor, such as after the death of Nero or in the wars when Severus defeated Niger and Albinus, even if traumatic for those who had to experience the wars, it was less damaging than the century of fighting and political instability that characterized Late Republican Rome. At the beginning of book 44, Dio makes it clear how he saw a monarch as a better solution than what he calls the role of the masses: 'and again, even if a base man obtained supreme power, yet he is preferable to the masses of like character, as the history of the Greeks and barbarians and of the Romans themselves testifies' (Dio 44.2.2).

Another reason why Dio favoured a monarchical constitution is that the political process was easier. The implementation of laws and decisions about where Rome should go to war or offer peace were determined by the emperor and members of his court. In a monarchy, laws would no longer meet resistance from the assemblies or the Senate, emerging from concerns that those behind the laws were seeking popularity from passing legislation that favoured the general public. As we shall see, democracy in its Republican form was, in Dio's eyes, a form of oligarchic tyranny where groups of senators and what Dio refers to as the 'dynasts', the most influential men in Late Republican politics, such as Sulla, Pompey and Caesar, held the city and its people hostage in their struggle for power.[3] In this political climate, the senators were unable to meet the basic needs of Rome's inhabitants. In an attempt to acquire as much power and prestige as possible, members of the elite lost track of what was in the best interests of the Commonwealth, and failed to provide the necessary stability to ensure Rome's inner peace and much-needed prosperity (Dio 57.37.3).

The failings of the democratic system

Dio's scepticism about democratic rule first appear in the opening of book 44, where the narrative breaks off to allow the historian's own thoughts on democracy, on what he calls Caesar's monarchy, and on the reason why he was murdered. On the choice between democracy and monarchy, Dio gives his readers the following observation of why one-man rule would always be the most stable form of government, not just in Rome but in most states.

> Democracy has a fair-seeming name and gives the impression of bringing equality to everyone through equal laws, but in its effects it in no way agrees with its title. Monarchy is the opposite – it is unpleasant to hear, but is the most serviceable form of government to live under. For it is easier to find one good man than many, and if even this seems to some people to be a difficult feat, the alternative must be acknowledged to be impossible; for the masses have no part in acquiring virtue.
>
> Dio 44.2.1–2

Over the subsequent passages, Dio moves on to assure his readers that success had always been greater under kings than under popular rule, and that failings and disasters happened less often in a monarchy than under what he tendentiously describes as mob-rule. When a democracy was prosperous it was only for a short period of time, and only until the people were numerous enough or influential enough to make demands in exchange for support. To Dio, in a state the size of Rome, harmony – that is inner peace and political stability – was unobtainable. As a result, the only way to ensure modesty or prevent unlimited ambitions, would be to abolish the race for prestigious magistracies and military commands altogether (Dio 45.3–5).

Dio is unfairly comparing monarchy or kingship, which earlier political thinkers such as Aristotle and Polybius would agree represent one-man rule in its finest form, with mob-rule the depraved version of the rule of the multitude (Aristotle *Politics* 3.8, 4.4, and Polybius 6.3–10). Dio would have been well aware that he was comparing different forms of constitutions at two different stages of development. Where monarchy represents one-man rule in its finest hour, in political thought mob-rule was, as Polybius would say, a depraved form of democracy (Polybius 6.4.4–5).

By comparing monarchy in its most stable form with the rule of the many in its most unstable stage, Dio distorts the discussion from the beginning, depriving his reader of a balanced analysis of the costs and benefits of the two forms of constitution. Despite the fact that he offers his own personal take on how political history develops, he still owes his thoughts on political theory to the writings of Plato, Aristotle and Polybius. Without being as explicit as Polybius, Dio sees constitutional history as a cyclical process where monarchical rule turns into a tyranny as the monarchs become too arrogant and self-righteous in their claim to power. Eventually the members of the political elite will replace the kings and rule as an aristocracy until they themselves turn greedy and overly ambitious, with little interest in what was in the best interests of the state. As a result, they have to give way to a more democratic form of constitution as the people assume real influence over the decision-making process.

However, in the way Dio shapes his argument, there is no moment in the history of Roman politics where the rule of the many offered a better alternative to monarchical rule. Up until the fall of Carthage, the Roman Republic was relatively free from civil strife and was politically stable. Because of the fragmentary state of books 1–21, it is difficult to know with certainty, but Dio seems to have viewed the constitution from the exile of the last king Tarquinius Superbus in the late-six-century BCE in terms of what Aristotle describes as a 'polity'. In one of the fragments that appears somewhere in the coverage of the Punic Wars, Dio describes how Rome was at its most stable.

> The Romans were at the height of their military power and enjoyed complete harmony among themselves. And so, unlike most people, who are led by pure good fortune to boldness, but by strong fear to mildness, at this time they had a very different experience. For the greater their successes, the greater discretion they had; against their enemies they displayed that daring which is a part of bravery, but toward one another they showed the mildness which goes hand in hand with good order. They used their power to exercise safe moderation and their orderliness to acquire true bravery; not allowing their good fortune to develop into arrogance or their mildness into cowardice. They thought that in the latter case discretion was destroyed by bravery and boldness by fear; whereas with them moderation was rendered safer by bravery, and good fortune firmer by good order. It was due to this in particular that they conducted the wars that befell them so successfully and administered both their own affairs and those of the allies so well.
>
> Dio frg. 52

Nevertheless, in the way Dio chooses to tell the story, the struggle for power, envy and fierce competition for power and prestige were always an integral part of Roman politics, even in the Early and Middle Republic. The difference was that a few qualified and modest men, and the threat of a powerful external enemy, were able to keep the elite reasonably united. However, the threat from the people's interference in the decision-making process and the loss of modesty among members of the elite were always laying just under the surface ready to flag when Rome was under pressure.

After having established that any democratic form of government would eventually collapse, Dio moves on to illustrate his point by describing why the coalition of senators killed Caesar, to whom Dio refers as the protector of the state, because prominent members of the Senate felt that Caesar's success and firm grip on power would repress their opportunity to shine. In Dio's account at the beginning of book 44, Caesar is not free from blame. The unstoppable urge for glory and pomp set him apart from his peers and the extraordinary honorary decrees helped to widen the gap between himself and the rest of the political elite.[4] They also paved the way for his premature death, and arguably the most devastating civil war in the history of Rome following the dictator's death in 44 BCE. Had the conspirators known the consequences of their acts, Dio speculates, they might not have murdered the man whose introduction of a new form of monarchy took Rome in the right direction. Here, it is necessary to acknowledge that Dio makes a deliberate choice in the narrative to present Caesar as a monarch and not explicitly as a dictator, a title he, at other passages, sees as a step towards tyrannical rule.

In Dio's mind, Caesar was foolish when desiring largely empty honours in the first place, and for believing they were somehow deserved. But Caesar's death and the outbreak of the civil wars were the responsibility of the conspirators and of a political elite who, by killing Caesar, threw Rome into a new round of war between citizens and a systematic cleansing of political opponents. To Dio, the death of Caesar marked the return of the tyranny of factions, where strong dynasts fought each other and the Senate to win supreme power and fulfill their own ambitions – ambitions that also applied to the second triumvirate formed by Octavian, Antony and Lepidus (Dio 48.34.1, 46.34.4, 47.39.2 or 55.2).

On the other hand, the Senate struggled to turn back the clock to a time where access to the political posts and military commands was more open and a matter for them and the assemblies. This was the reason why a coalition of senators killed Caesar, and the plan behind Cicero's mistimed attempt to use the veterans of Octavian and Caesar under his command to bring Antony, Caesar's second in command, to his fall (Dio 45.15.3–4). Also, it was precisely the ambition to rule and the urge for magistracies, commands against wealthy, resourceful and therefore also prestigious enemies, and the ultimate honour of celebrating victories with a triumph that encouraged the unhealthy political culture, where members of the elite broke the law and challenged the tradition to surpass each other.

Dio offers an almost structuralist explanation as to why Roman politics in the age of the Republic evolved in the way it did. Still in book 44, he describes how democratic forms of government could be reasonably successful until the moment when, as a result of the successes, the people grew more demanding.

> In fact, if ever a democracy has bloomed, it has in any case peaked for only a brief time, so long, that is, as they had neither the numbers nor the strength for arrogance to spring up among them as the result of good fortune or jealousy as the result of ambition.
>
> Dio 44.2.3

Later in the same paragraph, Dio makes the connection between conquest, wealth that was won in wars and the lack of modesty that led to uncontrolled ambitions, envy within the political elite and eventually to war between citizens. For once, Dio is very clear about how this is his own personal point of view.

> But for a city, not only so large in itself, but also ruling the finest and the greatest part of the known world, holding sway over men of many and diverse natures, possessing many men of great wealth, occupied with every imaginable pursuit, enjoying all imaginable

good fortune, both privately and collectively, – for such a city, to practise moderation under a democracy is impossible, and it is more impossible to be harmonious, unless they are moderate.

Dio 44.2.4

In other words, Rome was reasonably stable in the Early and Middle Republic because the Romans were still fully occupied with winning control over Italy and defending themselves against other Italian states and Carthage, particularly in the Second Punic War.

As we saw above, it was, according to Dio, with the fall of Carthage and the loss of an enemy strong enough to threaten Rome's very existence that the political culture started to degenerate (see above Dio frg. 52). This is a view he shares with other ancient writers, most noticeably, perhaps, Sallust, one of the few writers Dio actually mentions in the course of the work (Sall. *Cat.* 10–12), but also Velleius Paterculus and Tacitus who offer a similar analysis in the *Histories* (Vell. Pat. 2.1–2 and Tac. *Hist.* 2.38.3). It is particularly interesting how Dio's conclusion seems to differ from what we can draw from the narrative in the early books, where lust for power and personal ambition remain key elements and the underlying explanation of why the political elite acted in the way it did.

This sudden shift in the approach to Rome's political culture may have been a matter of style. By offering what is essentially a fairly celebratory claim for how Rome's success rested on a set of moral values where moderation was perhaps the most important, the degeneration of the political elite and the failings of a democratic form of constitution become even more pronounced as the narrative moves into the Late Republic.

In his coverage of Late Republican Rome, Dio follows what seems to be a generally accepted periodization in Roman historiography, where Tiberius Gracchus' election as the people's tribune in 133, and his death in what was the first incident of political organized violence, changed Roman politics forever. The Greek historian Appian, from the city of Alexandria in Egypt, offers a similar description of how Tiberius Gracchus' entrance on the political stage and his violent death marked a new age in Roman history, where inner strife and political violence became an integrated part of the decision-making process (App. *B Cic.* 1.2.1). Among the Latin authors, Velleius Paterculus and Tacitus offer a similar account about how violence all of a sudden was brought in as a tool in Roman politics (VP 2.3 and Tac. *Hist.* 2.38.1). Dio takes a step further and talks about a political climate that resembled war more than peace. After Marcus Octavianus and Tiberius Gracchus had fallen out with each other during Tiberius' attempt to redistribute the land Rome had confiscated from its enemies, warlike behaviour broke out in Rome when Gracchus' supporters and the gangs organized by members of the Senate fought on Capitol Hill before the vote was held.

> After that there was no semblance of moderation; but zealously vying to prevail over each other rather than to help the state, they committed many acts of violence as if in a despotism rather than a democracy, and suffered many unusual calamities as if in war rather than in peace. For in addition to their individual rivalries there were many who banded together and indulged in oppressive abuse and conflicts, not only throughout the rest of the city, but even in the Senate-house itself and the popular assembly, with the proposed law their pretext, but in fact they were making every effort in all respects not to be outdone by each other. The result of this was that none of the usual business was carried out in an orderly way and the magistrates could not perform their customary duties, courts came to a stop, no contract was agreed, and other sorts of chaos and disorder were rampant everywhere. They bore the name of city, but were no different from a military camp.
>
> Dio frg. 83.4–6

Again, Dio's comment on what characterized Late Republican Rome has also survived among the fragments. But even if the context is missing, it is sufficiently clear from the paragraph how the author viewed the last century of what he would refer to as democratic Rome. In Dio's eyes, Rome was hereafter brought to its knees by a political culture, where the Romans, without the threat from powerful external enemies, were free to use their elaborate resources and considerable military capacity to conquer as much of the known world as possible. The urge to surpass their peers now encouraged the elite to use violence in order to stay ahead – a view that unveils Dio's aristocratic belief and dismissal of the profound social problems in Late Republican Rome. Some of the politics that people voted for was, as we shall see in Chapter 2, a new fairer redistribution of the land, and protection against the raids of pirates on the coasts of Italy. These were laws that would have to be carried through the city's political institutions with force and stamina by some of Rome's most influential men, strong enough to challenge what would essentially be the entire political establishment. Even if Dio recognized the need for land reforms, it is interesting to note that Dio, who criticizes Rome's political elite for its inability to act on the city's pressing problems, never once sees the various issues from the point of view of the people.

For their part, the people carried a considerable responsibility for how Roman politics developed between the death of Tiberius Gracchus and the accession of Augustus. As Rome expanded and more and more resources were channelled into the city, competition between members of the political elite intensified. Gradually the people grew more demanding. In collaboration with the tribunes of the plebs, the popular assembly challenged the constitution in pursuit of what Dio saw as selfish and shortsighted decisions.

Monarchy prevails

In the narrative Dio offers, the crisis of Republican Rome culminates in 44 BCE with the murder of Caesar, which dissolves the first stable form of government that Rome had had for a long time. Dio describes the war between the different parties as the worst civil war in the history of the Romans, where all the contenders followed their own agendas with little thought as to what was in the best interests of the state. The members of the triumvirate, Lepidus, Mark Antony and Octavian, all hoped to win power for themselves and were all involved in gruesome acts of violence during the many years of fighting.[5] Octavian, Dio's favourite, was no less determined than his fellow triumvirs, and as we shall see in Chapter 2, from time to time no less brutal than his colleagues (Dio 47.1.1). But he comes across as different in how he wanted supreme power, not because he desired to rule or because he wanted power for its own sake, but because he hoped he would be able to punish Caesar's murders and bring much-needed stability to Rome. This claim is being made in the end of the book on Augustan Rome, where Dio draws up a conclusion of Augustus' importance for Rome and the Roman people.

> The Romans missed him greatly, not only for these reasons but also because by combining monarchy with democracy he preserved freedom for them and established order and security, so that they were free from the boldness of democracy and from the arrogance of tyranny, living in freedom and moderation and in a monarchy that held no terror; they were subjects of royalty, but without slavery, and citizens of a democracy, but without discord.
>
> Dio 56.43.4

Here, Augustus appears as a saviour figure who helped Rome and the Romans get back on track by ending civil war and by leading the city towards a better future. By introducing a form of monarchy where members of the elite were no longer able to pursue their own ambitions, Dio's Augustus freed the Romans from the terror of civil war and political instability. Octavian's role in the wars, gruesome as it was, is seen by Dio as an unfortunate but necessary evil to introduce the needed reforms to the constitution and, just as importantly, to recalibrate the political culture so that liberty and free competition would no longer be a part of Roman politics (Dio 56.41.2).

As in the books on Republican Rome, Dio organizes the coverage of Augustan Rome as a mixture of his own statements and conclusions, and fictitious speeches, where he offers points of view that might in all likelihood have been his own, and a narrative that supports his own approach to Rome's political history. His thoughts on how to organize the best form of monarchical government are laid out in book 52, where, in what is a fictitious dialogue between his friends Maecenas and Agrippa, he stages a scene where Octavian is listening to advice on whether to re-establish the republican form of government or introduce monarchical rule.[6]

In the form of government Maecenas suggests, influence from the masses should be kept to a minimum. The emperor should rule in cooperation with the best men across the empire – not only members of the Italian and Roman elite. How to organize that kind of government is described in the first paragraphs of Maecenas' answer to Agrippa.

> However, the other course would be honourable and useful both for you and for the city – that you should yourself, in consultation with the best men, enact all the appropriate laws, without any opposition to them or remonstration on the part of anyone from the masses; that the wars should be conducted according to your counsel, with all other citizens immediately obeying the commands; that the selection of the officials should rest with you and your advisers; and that you and they should also determine the honours and the punishments, so that everything that pleased you in consultation with your peers would immediately become law ...
>
> Dio 52.15.1–2

Dio moves on by letting Maecenas proclaim that military operations would be carried out more efficiently since decisions and preparation could be made in secrecy, and because those in charge would be elected as a result of skills and experience, not because the post was allotted to them or because they secured the command after a popular vote (Dio 52.15.3).

Not surprisingly, the decision-making process in a monarchy is also expected to be more efficient, leaving it more likely that the right choices are made. Dio draws a connection between one-man rule and a reduced risk of civil war before he has Maecenas remind the reader about the city's chaotic history.

> And so, business would be most likely to be managed correctly, neither referred to the popular assembly, nor deliberated upon openly, nor entrusted to men who have been summoned, nor exposed to the danger of ambitious rivalry; and we would enjoy our good circumstances, free from dangerous wars or in wicked civil strife.
> Dio 52.15.4

This risk of civil strife only to fulfil personal ambitions, Dio claims, was a challenge every democracy had to face. The only way to prevent politically motivated violence and civil war from happening was to introduce a form of constitution, where it was the responsibility of Octavian and the later emperors to show moderation and find ways to include the elites from across the empire with the qualities and the skills needed to assist.

Dio uses the analogy of a ship captain who holds the same course keeping the boat from drifting without direction. It is also up to Octavian to choose his own crew. In a number of passages, Maecenas suggests how his friend was to organize Rome's political institution. In terms of how to change the Senate, Maecenas offers the following advice.

> And so, I say first and foremost that you should choose and select carefully the whole senatorial body, since some who have not been suitable have, on account of factions, become senators; those of them who have some excellence you ought to retain, but the rest

you should let go ... Instead of them, introduce the noblest, the best, and the richest men you can, selecting them not only from Italy but also from the allies and the subject nations. In this way you will have many assistants and will keep in safety the leading men from all the provinces ...

Dio 52.19.1–3

A more systematic inclusion of members of the political elite would hardly have been a theme that any member of the political elite in Rome would have discussed in the early 20s BCE. It was not until emperor Claudius in 48 CE decided to offer men from the Gallic elite a seat in the Senate and not until the reign of the Flavian dynasty in the second half of the first century CE that the wealthy elite in Spain were added to the Senate in a systematic manner. What Dio hoped to achieve, instead, was to underline that the provincial elite was as capable and as natural a part of the political elite as Italian senators, who, in the Late Republic, were responsible for the chaos and instability that marked Roman politics up until Octavian's accession to the throne sometime between 29 and 27. However, it is worth keeping in mind that when Dio wrote his books on Augustan Rome, few in Rome would have disagreed with how men from the provinces were just as valued as members of the elite as the people from Italy. It was at a time when the emperors were of Spanish, African and Syrian origin and when Nerva (96–98), the last emperor of Italian origin, had ruled more than a century ago.

What Dio may have hoped to achieve was to promote a notion of how the ideal emperor was to take advice from members of the elite and therefore, in a sense, ruled on behalf of the entire empire. But also that such kinds of structure were already part of the mindset when the Principate was first introduced. Again, thoughts like these belong to a late-second- to early-third-century debate, where Greek intellectuals such as the orator and Aristides and Dio felt that they and members of the Greek elite more broadly had become, or were becoming, still more integrated in the empire's political establishment (Aristid. *To Rome* 59 and 63).[7]

However, there are also elements here to suggest that Dio felt a need to underline the importance of involving provincials in the decision-making process. The effort may be seen as an attempt to remind the emperor, but surely also members of the civic elite in the provinces, of the need to include civic elites in the administration, as this would be the only way to ensure that the government and the imperial administration would rest on loyalty from the provinces. Furthermore, and just as importantly, it was the only way to ensure a sufficient number of qualified men stepped onto the political scene in Rome and later took up the many different posts in the imperial administration. Dio's own role as governor and senator, and that of his father's, is here noticeable and it is perhaps an attempt to encourage other elites in the provinces to follow their example.

The idea that Octavian should select the members of the Senate himself raises another question: whether Dio actually believed that each new emperor was to choose his own senators, or whether Octavian (as a consequence of the civil wars, for which Dio blamed the Late Republican Senate) had to reorganize the council so that its members were men of honour with the necessary skills to serve as the emperor's loyal advisors. It is difficult to imagine that Dio would somehow envision a form of organization where each new emperor would dissolve the Senate after being announced as the new sole ruler. The chaos that this would imply when people lost their status, and the resistance and the competition among the political elite to be re-elected, would be difficult to handle, and the risk of new episodes of political violence and even civil war would be apparent.

What the historian may very well have suggested instead is a system where the emperor was to select all magistrates, both junior and senior posts, without popular vote or interference from the part of the Senate. This practice would then, in effect, abolish the element of competition for public office, and the emperor would hand-pick the people he felt were the most qualified to both carry out the administrative tasks tied to the various magistracies and serve as his advisors in the Senate. Ideally, this would ensure that the most eligible men would also be the men involved in the decision-making process. Maecenas moves on to suggest the following.[8]

> For I say that at home you should appoint only these offices, and that of consul, and these merely out of regard for the institutions of our fathers and to avoid the appearance of making a complete change in the constitution. But select all these men yourself and no longer commit the filling of any of these offices to the masses or to the people (for they will quarrel over them), or to the Senate (for the senators will then behave anxiously).
>
> Dio 52.20.2

Once again, Dio is concerned about the potential instability of Roman politics and offers a way to ensure that the responsibility remained in the hands of one man alone, as that kind of organization would be the only way to ensure that the elite maintained its focus on the administrative tasks and its new role as the emperor's advisor.

Seen collectively, the constitution that Maecenas proposes is one where the emperor held unrestricted powers. The implementation of new laws was the responsibility of Octavian and the later emperors. Their desires were in effect the law. It was their right but also obligation to select magistrates at all levels as well as the required commanders, without interference from the people or the Senate and therefore also every new member of the Senate. In return for these considerable powers, Maecenas suggests that Octavian – and future emperors of course – shows a considerable degree of modesty but also an awareness of the importance of listening to the thoughts and advice from what Dio describes as the best men from across the entire empire.

The senators, for their part, were to offer the emperor the best possible assistance as his loyal advisors without opposition, but it was the emperor's own responsibility to make sure that he arranged his way of ruling in a way that he listened to available advice. As the Senate had handed their powers over to the emperor, this meant that it was not their responsibility whether the emperor cooperated or not. The free political competition and the military or political result that members of the elite were able to pursue in Republican Rome, was now a thing of the past. Any advancement and any career in Rome, in the army or in the imperial administration, were the emperor's decisions alone, except in the few provinces where the Senate chose the governor.

In that light, it was fundamental that the emperor appeared modest and refrained from elevating himself too far above members of the political elite. He should not allow a cult to be consecrated in his honour, and he should find ways to give the senators a meaningful role to play in the daily administration, such as the obligation to serve as judges (Dio 52.35.1-6). What Octavian had introduced was therefore in a sense a form of monarchy, where the emperor ruled on a mandate granted to him by the people and the Senate. To prove that was the case, Dio staged a scene in the opening of book 53, set sometime at the beginning of the 20s, where Octavian steps in front of the senators to give a speech where he renounces the powers he received as triumvir (Dio 53.3-10). Octavian informs his fellow senators that he is about to hand over all of his powers and leave Roman politics behind. The way Dio set the scene, Octavian acts as a magistrate or general who at the end of his command is reporting back to the Senate before stepping down. Octavian informs the council how he has ended the civil war and that the men behind Caesar's murder have been punished. This allows the victorious triumvir to claim that he has fulfilled the task that he had been assigned, when together with Lepidus and Antony, his new allies, he took office in 43.[9]

Dio has Octavian underline that he never pursued power for its own sake but only fought to remove the enemies of the state. From here Dio moves on to describe how the senators begged Octavian to accept the role as sole ruler, either because they feared a new civil war – when they were to decide who was to follow Octavian – or because they agreed that monarchy was the most stable form of constitution available. Over the next passages, Dio describes how first the Senate and then the people granted Octavian *imperium*, and with that the command over the provinces in which the legions were stationed, which, together with the consulship, granted the victorious triumvir full control over the army (Dio 53.3–10). The speech in the Senate and the following vote in both the Senate and in the assembly, probably in the *comitia centuriata*, are important elements in Augustus' self-representation as well as in Dio's narrative of how Octavian received supreme power and his mandate to sole rule from the city's political institutions. In Dio's definition, Augustus was not a tyrant who won power by winning the civil wars but a legitimate monarch who ruled on a time-limited mandate and on behalf of both the people and the senators – who were free not to extend his power if they saw fit.

It is no doubt true that Dio's description of how Octavian states his own withdrawal from the political scene, in the opening of book 53, is a clever move on the author's part to show how the newly-returned triumvir shocked a nervous and exhausted elite into compliance. Dio lets his readers know that Octavian had no real intention to step down. Instead, he presents us with a manipulating emperor who tricked the Senate into offering him powers that were previously unheard of.

This has led scholars such as Bernd Manuwald to conclude that Dio's Augustus was an intelligent, manipulative autocrat who wanted supreme rule at any cost, largely from the moment he learned about Caesar's death, and that he was just as fixated on power and just as ruthless during the principate as he had been in the course of the civil wars. Manuwald suggests that Dio did not distinguish between the calculated and ruthless triumvir and the more including princeps as had previously been a common trend among modern scholars.[10] Manuwald is right, it is the same man Dio describes. The *princeps* Augustus was just as determined as the young triumvir who took Rome into new civil wars in order to secure supreme power. However, it was never Dio's intention to write panegyric. What he offers, instead, is a personal version of Rome's political history, where Octavian took power but only to save the state. The civil war was gruesome but necessary in order to free Rome from the chaos and tyranny of unregulated ambitions that had dominated Roman politics for more than a century. Dio tells his readers about how the Senate was placed under considerable pressure to offer the extraordinary *imperium* when Augustus threatened to lay down his triumviral powers; and he describes in detail how Octavian was not afraid of using excessive force if he thought it necessary, such as he seems to have done when he ordered the execution of several hundred Roman nobles at the fall of Perusia (Dio 48.15.1–6).

As we shall see, Dio seems to believe that Caesar's heir wanted supreme power, not for the sake of having sole rule but to reintroduce the monarchy that the dictatorship of Julius Caesar had provided and to re-establish the political stability that was taking shape after Caesar was voted dictator for life. Dio's Augustus is the political mastermind who did what was necessary to save the Romans and help the state back to its feet. He was brutal when he had to be, but as we shall see, it was necessary, just as the civil war he fought first against Caesar's murderers and later against Antony was an unfortunate but necessary means to save Rome and the empire from destruction. When Dio's Augustus manipulates the Senate to grant him excessive power, Dio believes it to be the right thing to do, as the vote allowed him to rule on a mandate from both the Senate and the people. Similarly, the execution of Roman senators and members of the equestrian order was unfortunate. However, excessive use of violence is, as we saw above, to be expected in civil wars.

Dio's coverage of the course of events by which Octavian was granted monarchical powers, gives the impression of a speedy process, where the Senate passes a vote that grants considerable powers to Octavian. However, this is not necessarily the case, and we should not accept the claim too readily for how in particular the Senate was generally open to monarchy, just as it is worth noticing how Dio leaves almost no room for any opposition.[11] Furthermore, it is also worth noticing that unlike in the account of how Pompey was granted the commands against the pirates and Mithridates – where Dio offers a rather detailed account of the process leading up to the decision in fourteen chapters in book 36 – the reader is offered very little reflection on how members of the Senate responded to the introduction of what was now a formalized monarchy.

In how he shapes the account of one of the most important moments in the introduction of the Principate, Dio leaves us with the thought that the decision to offer Octavian supreme power was one made in agreement, or at least that there was a consensus among the senators that monarchical rule was to be preferred over war and instability. Of course, Dio is dependent on the information offered by his sources, which in part would have been Augustus' autobiography and of course the *Res Gestae* (34). Suetonius is another writer Dio seems to have read closely, both on the events at Perusia and on how Octavian offered to lay down his powers some time following his return to Rome after the civil war (Suet. *Aug.* 28). Another source Dio would have read is Tacitus, whom he may be seen to have disagreed with, particularly on how to portray Augustus and the role he played in the history of Roman politics. Where Tacitus claims that Augustus was a tyrant who wanted power for its own sake, Dio offers a version of how Augustus had to fight the war in order to replace mob rule with monarchy to ensure stability and save Rome from dissolution.

The short underexposed coverage of this crucial moment in the history of Imperial Rome weakens the value of his testimony for how

Rome's political elite responded to Octavian, to his claim to power in the early 20s and to how the senators as a group perceived the shift in Roman politics. Instead, Dio may very well have overstated the support for Octavian and the decision to offer him considerable military powers, which allows our historian to draw the conclusion about how the elite and the Roman public acknowledged his effort in the civil war.

Another matter is that the speech Dio attributes to Octavian is fictitious – his readers would not have expected otherwise.[12] However, it is dubious that Octavian acted in the arrogant fashion Dio describes, or that he was as manipulative as he appears in the version that the historian offers. The choice of angle is difficult to follow. The threat that Octavian poses in his speech when he reminds the senators of how difficult and potentially dangerous democracy is, is staged as an attempt to dissuade the political elite from returning to a republican form of government.

However, there is every reason to assume that some kind of theatrical exchange of courtesies did take place. Octavian might very well have offered to give his powers back or at least made it seem that way. Suetonius mentions that Augustus thought about restoring the republic and that the triumvir gathered the senators to his house to fill them in on the state of the empire. In the end, Octavian decided not to lay down his powers because he feared for his life, and because he felt he deserved his new won position for as long as it offered the Romans a stable form of government (Suet. *Aug.* 28–29). It may well be the same tradition that has inspired Dio's version of what the victorious triumvir told the Senators. In any case, the Senate accepted the gesture only to return it by offering *imperium* and celebrating the generosity of the victor by offering him different extraordinary honours, including the name Augustus. It helps that we are able to follow this decisive moment in Rome's political history in the *Res Gestae* (*RG* 6, 7, 34). However, the episode in the way Dio chose to tell it makes more sense as another attempt to underline just how potentially unstable democracies were. The advice Octavian offers the senators on how they should keep away from the property of others and instead use their own money, and how they should not wage war on those who want peace, reflect, as we shall see in the next chapter, Dio's descriptions of how the republican Senate, driven by greed and ambitions, destabilized Roman politics.

The remarks that Dio has Octavian offer in his speech to the senators may also be read as a reminder to readers in Dio's own contemporary years, not to abolish monarchical rule – even if the emperor currently in power was unable to live up to his obligation to rule in a fair and inclusive manner. How Dio presents the speech after Octavian's return from the East, the triumvir would not have had all that knowledge to share of how to rule at a time of peace. On the other hand, there is every reason to believe that Octavian received his power formally after votes in the Senate and on the assembly as suggested in the *Res Gestae*. Dio is therefore not simply wrong or manipulative when offering the speech in the way he does. Instead, he balances the ambition to write the history of the age of Augustus with the hope to demonstrate how the monarchical form of government is the only reliable form of rule and therefore much to be preferred over any other kind of constitution. On the other hand, it is important to bear in mind that he uses the narrative to shape an Augustus who fits into the role as Dio's ideal of what defined the competent monarch and the best or most stable form of monarchy.

These thoughts on how to rule Rome in the best and most efficient way possible are likely to have emerged from Dio's own experience from Roman politics in the late-second and early-third century. As a senator newly admitted to the order, Dio sat through what was surely terrifying meetings and other public events, where Commodus, Septimius Severus and Caracalla threatened the senators to comply or did their best to humiliate them, their supposed peers and partners in the government. It is, therefore, not all that surprising that Dio remarks on how competent emperors should do everything in their power not to become personally involved in trials when the accused was tried for treason, or fall to the temptation to be vindictive or open to rumour and slander.

Dio's points of view about how no man had become a god by election or how the love and loyalty of one's subjects was more important than statues and shallow worship with divine connotation that is woven in to the speech of Maecenas, should also be read as a reminder that the emperor's approval of his own cult demonstrates his lack of modesty and self-awareness (Dio 52.35.5). On the other hand, Dio's thoughts on how the monarchy would always offer the most harmonious form of government exceeded what would be the current needs of a troubled senator who felt the threats of largely disappointing emperors. As we shall see in the next section, there is a paradox in how Dio proposes a form of monarchy where the emperor is allowed unrestricted powers at a moment in time where one despotic emperor followed the other. One explanation is the all-consuming threat of civil war, which when Dio entered the political scene was once again part of Roman politics.

There is no doubt that Dio feared war between citizens or that he would go a long way to avoid the stress and horror that followed. He describes in detail the trauma Roman soldiers went through when they fought friends and men with whom they had previously served (Dio 41.54.1–3). Dio also reminds his peers that the top of the community would always suffer from civil war – something he experienced himself when living in fear of who would be the next senator to be met with unreasonable allegations or when the fighting between Roman armies would take place in Italy or at the walls of Rome. But as we shall see, there was also another rationale behind the proposed form of monarchy and the unrestricted power that Dio would place in the hands of the emperor.

Another key theme in the second part of the *Roman History* is how the most qualified emperor would be the one with a proven record from years of experience from the Senate and the imperial administration, and that the most stable form of government in the history of Rome dates to the period between the accession of Nerva to the death of Marcus Aurelius – the age of the adoptive emperors – where the emperors were men who listened to the advice from their peers in the Senate and treated them with honour. This brings us to the question of in what way Dio differs from other political commentators in antiquity in his view of Roman constitutional thoughts. Essentially, all other political thinkers in Imperial Rome would agree that monarchical rule is the only form of constitution to ensure peace and stability. But where Tacitus and also Pliny the Younger seem to endorse a form of constitution where the Senate has a say in the decision-making process and is free to take part in the government, Dio insists that the only power that the senators should have is the right to advise the emperor before he makes the decisions (Plin. Pan. 66 and Tac. *Hist.* 1.2).

Tacitus and Pliny lived and wrote in the more peaceful early-second century, at a time where the accession of Trajan sparked renewed optimism among members of the political elite who felt they lived in times of liberty. They believed they had the right not only to speak freely but also, as expressed by the emperor himself, to play a more direct role in government. On the other hand, as we saw in the Introduction, Dio lived in a period marked by changing emperors, political instability and new rounds of civil war. In that light, he had no hope that the Senate would be able to share power with the emperor, as that was bound to restart the competition among its members, increase envy and hatred, and eventually spark new episodes of political violence.

In search of the ideal monarch

Dio's view of how the only suitable government was a form of monarchical constitution, where the emperor held absolute powers, is further underlined by the point of how even mediocre sole rulers were to be preferred over the rule of the many. But this should not be taken to mean that Dio somehow accepted the reign of despotic and largely uncommitted emperors like he believed Caligula (37–41), Nero, Commodus and the numerous young and untalented emperors of his own time to have been.

When read in their entirety, the books on the age of Imperial Rome unveil standards of how the emperors were to organize their government so that they were able to rule in a most efficient and stable manner. As we shall see in the remaining part of this chapter, and discuss further in Chapter 2, good government was in Dio's eyes a form of rule where the emperor was keen to allow the Senate a role by asking them for advice and by being open to the counsel they gave, which rendered the exchange of ideas and points of view more than a showcase or an illusion. But it also required that the emperors were chosen from among the most experienced senators who had already proved their worth as magistrates and commanders: men such as Vespasian (69–79), Nerva, Trajan, Hadrian (117–138) and Marcus Aurelius.[13]

The notion of a constitution where the emperor held unrestricted power and whose responsibility it was to choose magistrates, commanders and new members of the Senate, and to make sure that new laws were implemented, ties in to a form of political system where the emperors would belong to the most illustrious but also most tested part of the senatorial elite. If chosen from among the most competent of the senators, the emperor would represent the Senate, and as a former senator himself, the people of Rome and across the empire, and so represent the entire state. In that way of thinking, the Roman monarchy, or Principate as was the term used by the Romans, would be a form of representative monarchy where the emperor, the first citizen that is, ruled on behalf of and with a mandate from his subjects. As we saw in Maecenas' speech, in order to minimize the risk of civil war and ensure political stability, the emperor would need to have absolute power over the army, the appointment of magistrates, as well as the right to approve and implement new laws. But to Dio this was an acceptable arrangement so long as the monarch was a competent, fair and modest member of the political elite with the right qualifications to fulfil the considerable task it was to rule a state the size of the Roman Empire.

Dio's thoughts on what constituted the ideal monarch challenge the notion of dynastic succession, where a son or male relative of the current emperor followed in his footsteps no matter how young or inexperienced he was at the time of succession, or whether he was qualified, committed or largely indifferent to the tasks ahead of him. The key passage on how the emperor in power was to choose his successor among the most qualified senators over male relatives is from book 68, where Dio covers Nerva's adoption of Trajan.

> And so, Trajan became Caesar and later emperor, although certain relatives of Nerva were alive. But Nerva did not value family relationship above the safety of the state, nor was he less inclined to adopt Trajan because the latter was a Spaniard instead of an Italian or Italot, since no foreigner had previously held Roman power; for Nerva believed it necessary to consider closely a man's ability rather than his nationality.
>
> Dio 68.4.1–2

To be sure, Nerva did not have many alternatives and Trajan was not by any means a loving and grateful adoptive son, but one who played along, adding just the right amount of military force as the commander of the legions in Germania to ensure that he would be the preferred choice. Trajan never took Nerva's name and strongly underlined his loyalty to his biological father by making sure that he too was deified after his return to Rome.

Dio's favourable view on a form of succession where the next emperor in line was chosen from outside the emperor's family is an illusion with little basis in historical reality. No emperor from Nerva until Marcus Aurelius had sons of their own to follow them. If that had been the case, it is more than likely that they would have chosen their sons as their successor. Hadrian was Trajan's nephew and seems to have secured his own succession from an alliance he formed with Trajan's wife Plotina – who Dio says acted out of love. It is Dio who, in the opening of book 69, describes how Hadrian's accession to the throne was dubious (Dio 69.1–2).[14]

Hadrian was not singled out as his uncle's successor and had to use excessive force to pacify the protest from members of a Senate who only reluctantly accepted the new monarch. Finally, it was Marcus Aurelius who broke the practice when he gave the throne to Commodus, who would soon prove to be one of the most problematic and despotic emperors in Dio's lifetime. Our historian assures us that Marcus Aurelius did not know Commodus' true nature and that it was the young man's advisors who destroyed his character (Dio 73[72].1). However, it does not change the fact that it was Marcus Aurelius, one of Dio's favourite emperors, who reintroduced dynastic succession and put to rest the tradition of choosing the next emperor in line from among the senators.[15]

Dio's primary concern was not to offer a balanced account of Roman politics in the second century but a version where experienced senators ruled efficiently in respect and cooperation with the Senate. To have the message come across, Dio orchestrated a narrative where all the emperors from Nerva to Marcus Aurelius were highly capable and well-versed as regents. As we saw above, Nerva was old but he was the last emperor that Dio knew of who was chosen by his peers in the Senate, and he adopted Trajan because he was the most talented (Dio 63.1.1 and 63.4.1–2). Although Trajan had imperialistic ambitions, he was modest in nature, fair and attentive to the needs of the senators (Dio 63.6–7).

Hadrian might have plotted against the Senate when he assumed supreme power with the help of Plotina, and he was behind the murder of several senators and other men of talent because he envied them (Dio 69.3). However, he disciplined the army and did his best to secure the practice of non-dynastic succession when planning not only his own adoption of Antoninus Pius (138–61) but also who was to succeed him as the next emperor in line (Dio 69.21). Marcus Aurelius, whose learning Dio cherished, was the model emperor: wise, fair and talented. Dio offers no thoughts on whether the emperor was to blame for ending the practice of choosing the next emperor from among the most talented men in the Senate.

Even if highly tendentious at times, Dio's thoughts on how to organize the most stable form of government are a coherent account of how monarchy was the only real choice (at least in the case of Rome), but also under what kind of emperor the monarchical form of government would be most stable. The series of statements that we saw above show how he deemed democracy historically unreliable, as free political competition encouraged a political culture where members of the elite were forced to compete for popular support.

As human nature was predisposed for competition among individuals to supersede other members in the community, the urge for power and status in being the first would lead to a struggle between the most powerful members of society that eventually would end in violence and war. For that reason, monarchical rule was always to be preferred even if the emperor was of a modest talent, because even if he lacked the skills to rule or did not have the right character, the rule of one man was still less dangerous compared to free political competition, where the wealthy and influential dynasts used everything in their power, including privately recruited armies, to fight each other or to march on Rome to take what they believed and claimed to be their right to rule.

As we shall see in the next chapter, Dio was not satisfied with an arrangement where the emperor was responsible for the safety of the senators and that their status in society was upheld in the appropriate way. What he wanted was an emperor of experience – one who was chosen from among the most qualified senators with the necessary military and political experience – men such as Dio who had served in the imperial administration with years of experience form the Senate – not boys such as Nero, Elagabal or Alexander Severus who depended on their mothers or other women in their families, or were overly ambitious young adults, such as the tyrannical Caligula and Caracalla. In Chapter 2, the focus is devoted to how Dio shapes a narrative that demonstrates to his readers how unstable democracy was and how human nature was unable to handle political freedom or show the required modesty to govern in a fair and balanced way, where the needs of the state were more important than the interests of the individuals in power.

The search for the competent emperor continued throughout the books on Imperial Rome, where Dio uses a mixture of biographical writing and traditional narrative to underpin when Rome was blessed by the rule of a competent emperor and when that was not the case. There is in his writing an ambition to cover the history of Rome as accurately as possible, but it is also fair to say from the examples and angles he chooses that he was driven by a mission to prove to his readers exactly why monarchical rule was better than any other form of government. On the other hand, one also detects a well-meaning attempt to decide what constituted a successful monarch and a stable form of monarchical rule. Not surprisingly, few emperors lived up to the definition he offers. One of them was Vespasian, who in Dio's eyes was the first competent emperor after the death of Augustus forty years earlier. But before we turn to what made the first of the Flavian emperors so special, we start at the other end with Rome's first kings and a type of monarchy that was not to Dio's liking. As I have already said, Dio preferred any emperor, even Domitian or Caracalla, over the political chaos and civil war that in his eyes was the consequence of the free, unregulated competition and political liberty that characterized Republican Rome. Only a monarchy, Dio believed, was able to suppress the less attractive sides of human nature: the greed, envy and the urge for glory and prestige necessary to be first among one's equals.

2

Roman Narratives

When reading all the available books, fragments and excerpts of *Roman History*, it soon becomes clear how Dio believed that the urge to surpass one's peers had always been an integral part of Rome's history.[1] According to his understanding, competition for power and prestige, arrogance, envy and politically-motivated violence were at all times dominant features in Roman politics from the Regal Period to the struggle for supreme power in the age of the Severan emperors (Dio 39.26.1). Out of natural lack of modesty, humans would always do whatever was in their power to gain as much influence and as much praise as possible; Dio believes that a strong desire to rule and be first may be found in all communities and in all periods of time no matter who governed or what sort of constitution was in play (Dio frg. 5.12). Wherever a man was on the social ladder, Dio believed he would always compete to improve his own position as much as possible. The real challenge was the opposite – to show modesty and to retain focus on what would be in the best interest of the state.

Dio's thoughts on how modesty was a largely unobtainable virtue, particularly in a city such as Rome, are a general theme throughout the books on Republican Rome but especially on two occasions. The first example is from the end of book 37, where, after having described the formation of the first triumvirate, Dio mentions that the political elite showed no modesty and that essentially everyone in politics from that moment onwards was looking out for his own interests (Dio 37.57.3). The other example is as we saw earlier from the opening of book 44 where modesty in a state as large and resourceful as Rome, with the military potential that the Romans had, is said to be unobtainable as long as the state was ruled as a democracy (Dio 44.2.4).

As discussed in Chapter 1, Dio firmly believed that free, unregulated competition between members of the political elite and the selfish struggle for political power would only be checked or limited if access to military forces, victories and political posts were tightly regulated by a single competent ruler. He was to use the political and military rule of only one man and be the one responsible for implementing laws and delegating military and political tasks to the most qualified individuals among the senators. In Dio's mind, it would always be members of the Senate, just as the emperor should always pay the utmost attention to demonstrate the most vigorous form of modesty in order not to awaken the envy and ambitions of his 'former' peers.

The following discussion focuses on Dio's thoughts on monarchical rule versus democracy from the Regal Period to his own time, and addresses the question of how Dio writes a narrative to support his notion of the ways powerful men would always strive to outdo their peers to gain as much influence and resources as possible. To demonstrate his hypothesis, Dio offers his readers a version of Roman history where an urge for power and prestige and a readiness to use every means available to fulfil personal ambitions remained the dominant factor in Roman politics. In the course of his narrative, Dio shows how kings and usurpers fought to win and to keep supreme power, and how the members of the political elite in the Early and Middle Republic did everything in their power to manipulate the Senate and the people to assume and maintain their position in the centre of Roman politics.

The way Dio describes it, the Early and Middle Republic come across as more stable periods, at least from an inner political point of view, than those of the early kings and Late Republican Rome.[2] This has led to the assumption among modern scholars and historians from antiquity that Rome was less troubled by inner strife and so was a less violent place. Livy and Dionysius of Halicarnassus offer what is often a version of events that is less violent, even if they are to be described as tense or as a moment of political strife (*stasis* in Greek).[3] Other ancient historians saw political violence as a Late Republican phenomenon such as the first-century historian Velleius Paterculus and the second-century historian Appian. Appian dates the first real incident of political violence to the re-election of Tiberius Gracchus as the people's tribune in 133 (Vell. Pat. 2.2.1–3 and App. *B Civ.* 1.2.1). As we saw in Chapter 2, Roman politics was arguably less turbulent from the late-sixth century to the election of Tiberius Gracchus in 133 BCE, than the 100 years between the death of Gracchus to the late 30s when Octavian defeated Cleopatra and Mark Antony at Alexandria, and ended fourteen years of war between the Romans. What Dio offers in his study of early Rome is a picture of how politics in the Early and Middle Republic were characterized by the same urge to represent Rome, and a strong ambition to be the general that defeated the city's enemies – sentiments and ambitions that stirred the political decisions that were made.[4]

In the books on Late Republican Rome, Dio offers a narrative of how Rome hid its first real low points when the political elite proved incapable of governing in a way where the needs of the Commonwealth were prioritized over the ambitions of individual members of the political elite. Dio's is a dramatic account of the way the political elite lost all sense of moral direction and how the unregulated competition of the many different members of the senatorial class led to violence between citizens that not only threatened Rome's position as a leader in the Mediterranean but the city's entire existence. With Octavian's victory in the civil wars (43–30), Rome was offered a new start. The city's first man was able to ensure stability, and under the new regime Rome was relatively free from individual ambitions and competition for power. That changed in part in the imperial period. Rome was once again in the hands of men with considerable ambitions and an urge to rule at any cost, driven by the almost unlimited powers and the enormous wealth that was available to the emperor. This is particularly obvious in the accounts of emperors such as Caligula, who spent considerable sums of money on gladiatorial games and worked actively to supress the Senate (Dio 69.2.5). The same picture is available in Dio's book 66, where he describes this period as Domitian's terror regime. Domitian murdered his brother Titus (79–81) to replace him as emperor and prosecuted numerous senators in what is best described as mock trials (Dio 66.20.2). Another example of a young and overly-ambitious emperor is Caracalla, who murdered his brother Geta in the arms of his mother Julia Domna, simply to assume supreme power. Caracalla was yet another example of a young emperor who suppressed the Senate and treated its members with contempt, leaving the senators in a state of fear and outside the political decision-making process (Dio 78[77].2 and 78[77].17.3–18.1).

As we shall see in the last part of this chapter, what kept Rome on track were the emperors who took it upon themselves to lead the city and the empire in cooperation with what Dio describes as the best men, the senators who had come to Rome to take part in the government as its loyal advisors. However, the risk of politically-motivated murders carried out by tyrannical leaders, ambitious and hateful members of the political elite and new civil wars fought between pretenders to the throne were always potential risks that members of the elite, men such as Dio, had to look out for. As we saw in Chapter 1, Dio believed that a monarchy would reduce that risk of chaos and civil war, even if the emperors' qualities as leaders were debatable (Dio 44.2.1). It is interesting to note that not all types of monarchies were to Dio's liking. The kings in the Regal Period did not, in general, meet the criteria for what Dio would define as the ideal kind of absolute ruler. They were, for the most part, overly ambitious and eager to rule because they desired power for their own sake and they lacked the modesty needed to slow down the aspiration of their peers. In other words, they were not examples to follow.

Tyrants and kings

In his coverage of the Regal Period, Dio would have relied on the existing accounts of Livy and Dionysius of Halicarnassus and a variety of other sources.[5] But instead of offering a version that aligned with the existing tradition, Dio offers an account that ties in to his overall interest of what constituted good monarchical government. These were standards only a few of Rome's first monarchs were able to meet.[6] Apart from Romulus the founder of Rome and Numa, who gave the Romans their gods and a number of the most important priesthoods, and in addition the means to live in peace with themselves and their neighbours, Dio describes most of Rome's earlier kings as men of little modesty fixated on how to become Rome's next sole ruler. The reign of most of the kings was often characterized by what Dio saw as an arrogant attitude to the city's political institutions, laws and the traditions that regulated political life in early Rome. Several of the later kings manipulated their way into power or benefitted from violent attacks on their predecessors.[7]

Dio's focus on the arrogance of power is apparent right from the start of the *Roman History*. Romulus is criticized for ruling without listening to advice from the members of the Senate whom he treated disrespectfully when they reminded him how it was the practice to seek consensus before the fate of hostages was decided. In a passage that survives among the fragments, Dio has the king come across as a leader who chose to insult rather than cooperate with the senators.

> Senators, I have selected you not so that you might rule me, but so that I might instruct you.
>
> Dio frg. 1.11

Here, Romulus is presented as the archetypal ruler who wanted power for himself and did not care to include the senators in his decisions – such figures are frequent in Roman politics. What Dio is after here is not an attempt to show that a democratic form of government would be better, where the senators are offered equal powers, but to demonstrate that Romulus turned tyrannical when he reminded the senators too bluntly that they were his subjects, and so neglected the advice and the support real cooperation with his peers would have offered him as a monarch.

King Tarquinius Priscus who is said to have ruled in the late-seventh and early-sixth century is described in a more positive light. Unlike Romulus, he is said to have proved more attentive to the needs of the people and the Senate, and was recognized as reasonably respected. He possessed some of the qualities cherished by Dio when he shared his success with others but took any blame that might come upon himself, or when he listened to criticism from others without feeling any anger (Dio frg 9.2–3). Priscus had the right qualities as a king but his road to power was characterized by lying and deceit. In Dio's version after the death of his predecessor, Ancus Marcius, Priscus manipulated the Senate to allow him to act as regent for Ancus' sons (Zonar. 7.8). His grip on power was further strengthened when he deliberately failed to prepare Ancus' son to take over and when he gave Servius Tullius, the son he had with a slave woman, an influential political position in his government. Priscus was later killed by a coalition where Ancus' sons were involved in an act of violence that brought Tullius into power (Zonar. 7.8). He also acted as regent now for Priscus' sons, whom he predictably made little effort to promote. Dio points towards how Priscus favoured the people with land and by distributing other forms of wealth, and he mentions that it was this king who introduced the patron–client relationship by enforcing freed slaves to be bound to their former masters. Priscus is said to have promoted liberty to such a degree that when the senators questioned his right to rule, he was voted king by the people (Zonar 7.9).

Dio's story of how Priscus became king by popular vote differs from Livy's notes on how kingship was not bestowed upon Tullius and may not be what happened (Livy 1.41 and 1.46). However, how Priscus become king need not concern us here. Neither Livy nor Dio would have been able to know with any kind of certainty. More interesting is that Dio balances his account of how the two kings ruled the Romans. We hear how both Priscus and Tullius came to power by manipulating the Senate to offer them the role as regents but also both of them apparently ruled in ways that benefitted the state and the people living in the city. But at the same time, Dio also shows the urge for power that made even some of the more inclusive and righteous kings cheat their way to the throne, and how they too were happy to break both laws and conventions to fulfil their own ambitions and acquire supreme powers.

It is when Servus Tullius is killed by Tarquinius Superbus, the king's younger half-brother, and the king's own daughter Tullia that Rome in the Regal Period hits rock bottom, as the city experienced the first real period of full-blown tyrannical rule. Dio describes Tarquinius' regime of terror in the following way.

> When he had made sufficient preparations to rule over them even against their will, Tarquinius first arrested the most influential of the senators and then of the others, putting many to death publicly, when he could bring some plausible charge against them, and many others secretly; and he banished some.
>
> Dio frg. 11.2

From here, Dio moves on to describe how Tarquinius killed numerous illustrious men out of fear, hatred and envy. He then moves on to show that the new king tried to abolish the Senate altogether because he apparently believed that every gathering of men, particularly of men with authority, was potentially dangerous to the rule of what is referred to as a tyrant.

When we read Dio's thoughts on the Regal Period together, the account he offers is one where personal ambition and lust for power at almost any cost dominates decisions. All the kings, except perhaps Numa, had to kill or manipulate their way into power, and they were willing to sidestep or humiliate the Senate in order to fulfil their own ambitions to be first among equals. Some of the kings – Numa, Priscus and Tullius – ruled in harmony with the people but Priscus and Tullius both had to use their position at the court to move legitimate sons out of the way to secure sole rule for themselves. Violence, greed and a persistent urge to be first, sometimes in modesty and in conviction that the subjects would remain loyal but often in fear of opposition, continued as dominant factors in Roman politics.

A few good men

Politically organized violence and war between citizens was not an integrated part of Roman politics until Late Republican Rome, Dio still saw unmanaged ambition as an integral part of human nature and therefore as the key element in Rome's political culture – also in the otherwise less turbulent Early and Middle Republic. The quest for power, fame and glory, and the desire to be the Roman general who defeated Rome's resourceful enemies such as Veii or Carthage, continued to be part of the decision-making process. This remained a strong incentive for members of the elite, even if supreme rule was not really an option other than in the instances where Rome elected a dictator for six months at a time.

One example is the story of the general Marcus Furius Camillus whose success on the battlefield sparked considerable envy among his fellow senators who used the power of a frustrated but ill-advised public to have him expelled from Rome. According to Dio, there was no reason for Camillus' exit other than an envious attempt to make up for the fact that the rest of the Senate was surpassed by the glorious victory against the Etruscan city Veii, Rome's mortal enemy par excellence. Another cause of envy was when Camillus managed to secure the surrender of the city of Falerii when the general, in a sign of good faith, returned the city's children to their parents in the besieged city after they were delivered to the Roman army by a school teacher who was hoping to benefit from the gesture (Dio frg. 24.2–6 and Zonar. 7.21).

In Dio's view, Camillus was not exiled because he broke any laws. The people were unhappy that the soldiers were not allowed to raid Falerii and frustrated that one-tenth of the spoils from Veii were handed over to the oracle in Delphi. They acted out of greed and out of the feeling that they had been deprived of the opportunity to loot the Faliscans and of a larger part of the spoils from Veii. For their part, members of the Senate remained passive, feeling a sting of jealousy when they saw how Camillus celebrated a spectacular triumph in Rome.[8] A similar example is found in Dio's coverage of the Middle Republic and the Second Punic War, when the dictator Quintus Fabius Maximus agrees to share his command with his master of horse and second-in-command Marcus Minucius Rufus in order to meet a wish from the people. Fabius is here portrayed as the bigger man, one of a few good leaders such as Camillus, who aspire to do what is in the best interests of the state and to serve the city's political institutions loyally. It proves to be the wrong decision to allow Rufus to share the high command. The ambitious master of horse loses when he moves out to face Hannibal but the Fabius whom Dio describes follows the people as the loyal magistrate he was (Dio frg. 57.16).

The story holds all the important features of Dio's history of Roman politics in the age of the Republic. Rufus' urge to be the general who defeats Hannibal is part of a human quest to succeed but ends up causing defeat because the decision to move out was determined by ambition. The whole episode ends up as a setback for the Romans. It is a classic example of how Dio saw ambition and lack of modesty as the cause of short-term decision-making and the reason why democracy was unable to ensure stability in Rome. As we saw in Chapter 1, Dio believed that the systematic use of violence as a tool to win political struggle characterized the Late Republic, beginning with Tiberius Gracchus' attempt to be re-elected as tribune of the people (Dio frg. 83). However, that violence was a part of Roman politics in the Early Republic is another point Dio returns to, such as when he describes that in their struggle with the plebs, the patricians used wars against foreign enemies as a means to keep the public busy, with no time to push for more political rights. Dio also mentions that the patricians secretly killed the most outspoken members of the plebs, and several tribunes were killed by the masses for not pursuing a policy that was in their best interests. The struggle for legal rights continued to dominate the decision-making process up to the point where Rome was losing its ability to fight its enemies with the force it once had (Dio frg. 22 and Zonar. 7. 17).[9]

The conclusion Dio offers remains the same. Democracy is too unstable to provide stability. Much unnecessary energy was being wasted on internal strife and the struggle to obtain more political rights. In order to hold on to their privileged position and a firm grip of power, the patricians murdered the most persistent members of the plebs and threw Rome into wars that were designed to occupy the people and keep them away from the struggle for more political influence. Dio recognizes how the Roman Republic was from time to time blessed with the leadership of men of quality and high-moral standards, which together with a series of existential wars kept the Roman elite reasonably united. But Roman politics was still determined by people's individual ambitions to surpass their peers and to be the ones who won the most prestigious wars. Commands they would soon prove ready to kill to obtain. Their victims were not only their immediate opponents but also innocent people in Rome and the soldiers in the armies whom they used to fight each other on the battlefield.

Democracy fails

As shown in Chapter 1, Dio describes the Late Republic as a time when war and political violence became a fully integrated part of Roman politics. The political system was dysfunctional, and life in the city resembled that of a military camp. Members of the political elite used the armies and the Roman people as tools in the struggle to win as much power and prestige as possible. One of the claims Dio makes is that essentially no members of the elite were in politics for reasons other than to do what was in their own best interests, except Cato the Younger. But it is however worth noticing that Cato, a righteous man in Dio's narrative who did his best to speak up against more ambitious men such as Pompey and Caesar, comes across as a man who falls short of his own ideals (Dio 37.57.3). Not only was he unable to make a difference in his opposition against Caesar when the latter moved forward with his land reform, but Cato became what is merely a parenthesis in Rome's political history. In the way Dio shapes his story, Cato lost his integrity when he opposed Caesar, not because he found any fault with the reform or did not recognize the need to do something about the concentration of land, but because he feared that Caesar would become too popular should he manage to carry through the bill (Dio 38.3).

To prove his hypothesis of how no member of Rome's politics was doing what was in the best interests of the Commonwealth, Dio draws up a narrative that focuses almost exclusively on how Rome's elite fought for power and influence over the decision-making process. To show that democracy was both chaotic and dangerous, Dio devoted nine books, 36 through to 44, to examples that illustrate how the most influential men in Roman politics promoted their own interests but also how hard they had to fight to maintain their hard-won position in the war zone Roman politics was turning into.

Dio's description of the political climate in Late Republican Rome makes it clear that violence and strife between members of the political elite intensified as the political culture degenerated and forced those involved to be still more ruthless and uncompromising in the attempt to stay in power or to make their way to the centre of the decision-making process. As we shall see, Dio believed that the result of what he saw as unmanaged competition, and the influence of the people, was a stage of continuous civil unrest culminating in three full-scale civil wars in the course of just five decades. Each war had devastating consequences for Rome, either because the wars were fought in Rome or in central Italy, or because Roman soldiers were forced to fight and kill each other, or because fighting between citizens unleashed an almost unparalleled hatred, similar or worse than the feelings known from wars between foreign enemies (Dio frg. 83.2–4 and Dio frg. 109).

Even if the fighting following the attempt of Tiberius Gracchus to win a second term as the people's tribune for 132 was hardly a war, Dio still characterized the armed clash between members of the Senate on the one side and Tiberius and his supporters on the other, as war or war-like behaviour. The text is heavily fragmented and it is from the historian Appian and the moral philosopher Plutarch that we have information that allows us to reconstruct what happened when the two parties fought each other on Capitol Hill (App *B Civ.* 1.16 and Plut. *Ti. Gracch.* 16–20).

As part of his programme, Dio describes how Tiberius Gracchus proposed a law that would allow a redistribution of Rome's public land to Roman citizens in the army (Dio frg. 83.7). The bill passed with difficulties and not without bending the laws. By the end of

Tiberius' term as tribune it was clear that the law might never be put into effect if Tiberius was not in office to oversee the implementation. It is here, at this moment, Tiberius and members of the public try to force through a second term as tribune and Dio describes how the entire family becomes involved.

> And when not even this proved of advantage to him and he was near the end of his term office (after which he would be immediately exposed to his enemies), he tried to secure the tribuneship for the following year also, together with his brother, and to appoint his father-in-law consul, not hesitating to say anything or promise anything to people.
>
> Dio frg. 83.8

Re-election as tribune two years in a row was against the law, which was the excuse members of the Senate used to kill the ambitious tribune and some of his supporters publicly. Dio recognized the need for a land reform (Dio 38.1–4). However, he offers his readers a rather negative portrait of Tiberius where he comes across as a mere revolutionary with little interest in the question of public land as such. Instead, the tribune is seen to have proposed a bill that he knew would earn him considerable popular support that he could later use to acquire an even stronger position in the centre of Roman politics (Dio frg. 83.3). Dio emphasizes how Tiberius turned towards the plebs when he was not awarded a triumph for his role in the war against the Numantines, which made him realize that his chance of becoming leader (something Dio says he wanted at any price), would require the support of the people.

The way Dio covers Tiberius' land reform is typical of how he works as a historian. He acknowledges that the problem of land concentration was real enough. However, in the brief text that survives, he never stops to consider whether Tiberius' intention was a sincere attempt to solve a pressing social and military dilemma or whether it would have been possible to redistribute the land with the Senate as his partners. It is interesting to note that Appian also agrees that Tiberius was ambitious, but he is not judging the tribune in the same way, and describes how the people rightly feared that the land reform would be abolished if their champion was not re-elected (App. *B Civ.* 1.9; 1.12; 1.14).

The first clash between Roman armies dates to the 80s, where Sulla and Marius fought each other for the supremacy of Rome. It was the first time Roman armies met one another on the battlefield, and the first time a Roman commander led his soldiers into Rome and allowed them to raid its people as if it was a foreign city. The war fell in two phases. The first phase dates to the beginning of the decade, with the competition between Sulla and Marius for the command against Mithridates, the king of Pontus and one of Rome's most resourceful enemies in central Asia Minor. The second phase dates to the second half of the 80s when Sulla returned from the First Mithridatic War (89–85) and marched on Rome against Marius and his supporters who in his absence had taken the city and declared him an enemy of the state.

At the beginning of the decade, as one of Rome's client kings in the region, Mithridates had managed to defeat two Roman armies, conquer the newly founded province of Roman Asia and, together with most of the Greek cities, carry out a massacre of the Romans and Italians in the cities of western Asia Minor. Marius had already set his eyes on a war against Mithridates, hoping that a victory against the king would allow him to regain some of the political momentum he had lost when as consul in the year 100 he had proved unable to provide the land that he had promised his soldiers after the war against the Teutones. However, as the result of his success in Rome's war against its Italian allies in the late 90s, Sulla obtained from the Senate the command against Mithridates.

Marius referred the question to the *comitia tribute,* and with help from the tribune Publius Sulpicius Rufus, the assembly passed a law that recalled Sulla's command and made Marius the general to fight the Pontic war. That law was legally binding by comitia tributa's right to pass laws and would override the decisions made by the Senate. Sulla, for his part, did not accept the outcome of the vote and led his army into the city where he fought Marius and his supporters in the streets of Rome forcing them to flee the city. He then settled the affairs in Rome before he turned in the east on Mithridates whose generals had just conquered Athens.

Dio's coverage of the war between Sulla and Marius is fragmented, with no narrative left of the events leading up to Sulla's march on Rome or of how the two generals fought inside the walls. Instead, Dio's account picks up after Sulla had won control over the city and Marius had been forced to flee the capital. What is left of Dio's text still unveils a depraved political climate where the ambitious consul Lucius Cornelius Cinna tried to interest Sulla in the command against Mithridates. Cinna's objective was not to find an experienced general for the coming war against a resourceful enemy but to have Sulla leave the capital so that the consul could fill the vacuum. For his part, Sulla thought that the war on Mithridates was necessary and he was keen, Dio assures us, to bring the troublesome king to a fall. Sulla's urge for the prestigious victory made him underestimate Cinna's ambitions, and as he moved out to conquer Pontus, Cinna brought the Marians back in to the city (Dio frg. 102).

The scenes Dio describes are brutal. The Marians ordered their troops to murder anyone in the city but particularly those who were wealthy, and as many of Marius' political enemies as possible. The general then tells his troops to kill and abuse Roman women and children as if they were foreigners. The soldiers, who were Roman citizens too, were allowed to raid the city for five days and nights (Dio frg. 102.10). It is worth noticing here how Dio's description of the brutality and terror Marius unleashed on his fellow citizens resembled the mechanism behind the war in Corcyra as described by Thucydides.

Here the people and the aristocracy fought over the control of the city and as part of the war committed numerous atrocities and unleashed hatred and envy between the social classes in the city (Thuc. 3.81–85).[10]

The coverage of the mechanism behind the killing of fellow citizens ties into the notion that wars between fellow citizens were often more gruesome than fighting between foreign enemies. One of the reasons why is that war between kinsmen was often more personal and shocking to begin with, and so also potentially more traumatizing for those involved. When Sulla returned victorious from having defeated Mithridates, the violence continued. The text we have is devoted to Sulla's proscriptions of his political enemies. Proscription is a legal arrangement where individuals are listed as outlaws, with death sentences hanging over them and their possessions being the property of the state. From here Dio moves on to describe the way in which Sulla's associates were hunting both their own enemies and those of their leaders across all of central Italy. Envy and hatred were once again part of the reason why people were killed in great numbers, often as they had sought protection at sanctuaries or after they had surrendered to their pursuers (Dio frg. 109).

Political violence, massacres and raids on the capital ordered and carried out by Roman citizens were now an established part of Roman politics. In Dio's account of the unstable nature of Rome's democratic constitution, the scenes in Rome in the late 80s offer a new momentum in his narrative of how Roman politics was falling victim to greed and personal ambitions to secure commands against prestigious enemies, and the urge to have power for its own sake. As we reach the part of Dio's text that has come down to us in larger chunks, it becomes clearer that what he aims at is to show that members of the elite were doing everything in their power to stay ahead. For those who were not to be counted among the most influential members of the elite, the objective was to do whatever they could to narrow the gap between themselves and the more successful individuals among their peers.

The focus is on how what Dio refers to as the dynasts, men such as Sulla, Pompey, Caesar and Octavian, used their large popularity and military force to pursue their own interests, often against Rome's laws and political conventions.[11] Some of the key figures in Dio's analysis of the political crisis in Late Republican Rome were the people's tribunes who, like Tiberius Gracchus, were highly-privileged members of the political elite who nonetheless counted among the plebs. As we shall see, the most ambitious of the people's tribunes is seen by Dio as one of the main reasons why Roman politics was as chaotic as it turned out to be from the early 60s onwards down to the moment Caesar acquired supreme power as dictator for life.

This alliance between dynasts and ambitious tribunes is laid out most vigorously in the coverage of how in the 60s Pompey was voted two campaigns: one against pirates in the Mediterranean in the year 67, and again the year after one against Mithridates – who continued to pose a threat to Roman interests in Asia Minor. After his consulship in the year 70, when Pompey reversed Sulla's law that took away the tribunes' right to lay new laws before the *comitia tributa*, the now ex-consul was ready for new military tasks. The right moment came when pirates in the Mediterranean Sea became self-confident enough to raid the Italian shores and threaten not only the immediate safety of travellers and people living on the coast but also the corn supply to Rome.

The problem was well known and other Roman generals had been given considerable resources to deal with it but largely without success. Following up on the new incidents of pirates' activity, the tribune Aulus Gabinius suggested that one of the ex-consuls, in effect Pompey, should be given previously unseen powers to wage war on the pirate communities across the Mediterranean Sea. When considering the motives behind the proposal, Dio assures us that the tribune was not acting out of concern of the safety of the people.

Either he had been prompted by Pompey or otherwise he wished to please him (for he did not do this out of love for the common wellbeing, for he was a most evil man). His plan was that one general should be chosen from among the ex-consuls to have full power against all the pirates, to have command for three years and have the use of a huge force, with many lieutenants. He did not mention Pompey's name directly, but it was clear that as soon as the populace heard of any such proposition, they would choose him.

Dio 36.23.4–5

In the following passages, Dio describes how all of Rome, except the senators who would prefer to suffer the raids than to see that kind of power in the hands of Pompey, supported the plan. However, the opposition among the senators was so pronounced that Gabinius was nearly killed at the meeting where the proposal was discussed (Dio 36.24.1). In response to the opposition, the people attacked those senators who sat with them on the assembly and would have killed them had they not quickly moved out of the way.

The incident is revealing of how Dio saw the shortcomings in Rome's republican constitution. He agreed that the threat from the pirates was real and had to be dealt with. Gabinius proposes Pompey either as part of a plan that they had made together or as an attempt to catch the attention of the popular ex-consul. The proposal won a positive reception from the people but was met with resistance from the Senate, where the members were not prepared to give Pompey that kind of power. In the version Dio offers, Rome's political institutions were unable to make a decision because it would be influenced by jealousy on the part of the senators who feared that Pompey would become too dangerous and popular with the people in Rome if left with that kind of military power and won the war against the pirates. That the decision was carried through, in the end, was only because of the senators' fear for what seems to have been a very real threat from the public who were persuaded by the ambitious tribune who, at the same time, used the opportunity to enhance his own position. It is worth mentioning here that Gabinius was one of the men who later held important military posts in Pompey's war against Mithridates and in the following campaign in the Near East. However, it needs to be remembered that senators looked bad when they tried to solve the problem by having Gabinius killed.[12]

Another incident where Pompey's military ambitions were carried through the assembly on the initiative of one of the tribunes, is when the successful general was voted the command against Mithridates. This decision made by *comitia tributa* meant that another of Rome's generals, Lucius Lucullus, was recalled after he had made considerable progress against Mithridates since the beginning of the war in 74. By the time Pompey reached the shores of Asia Minor in 67, Lucullus was beginning to lose momentum and he had just suffered a considerable defeat with the loss of several thousand soldiers and numerous military tribunes. Once again, Dio describes a process where the decision was not made on a political and military rationale but to fulfil what is described as a personal agenda of the tribune Gaius Manilius who was facing trial after he had proposed to offer freed slaves the right to vote. Dio relates a desperate attempt to save the situation.

> Then, in fear because the plebs were extremely angry, at first he attributed the idea to Crassus and some others, but when no one believed him, he flattered Pompey even in his absence, especially because he knew that Gabinius had the greatest influence with him. He offered him command of the war against Tigranes and that against Mithridates, and the governorship of Bithynia and Cilicia at the same time.
>
> Dio 36.42.3

Dio moves on to describe how the proposed change of command was met with considerable resistance among members of the aristocracy. Nevertheless, Manilius' proposal carried the day when the people voted in favour of the law even though they had previously sent a delegation to Pontus in recognition of how Lucullus had already won the war. We hear how Caesar and Cicero, whose speech in favour of the law has come down to us as the *pro lege Manilia*, supported the proposal, not because they thought it was in the best interests of the state but because they hoped they would benefit from supporting Pompey, and Caesar is said to have hoped that in the future he would be able to use the assembly in similar ways.[13]

Our historian is not being entirely honest. Lucullus may have called upon the Senate for them to verify Mithridates' defeat. But before the delegation could reach central Asia Minor, Lucullus, or more correctly his army without him leading it, had suffered defeat at the hands of Mithridates and his son-in-law Tigranes, the King of Armenia. Mithridates had regained control over the core of his kingdom and Tigranes had taken possession of Cappadocia. Lucullus' soldiers were losing faith and his ability to win the war was dramatically reduced. In other words, Pompey who had vanquished the pirates after just a few months, was conveniently in the region and the obvious choice to carry on the war. This would not have been unknown to Dio, who chose to tell the story in a way where the focus was on personal motives and individual ambitions rather than on military reasoning.

Pompey's unlimited urge for military honour was seen as the reason why he would push for the command in a war that was already won, and why he would accept the offer from a tribune, who by stirring up the political waters in Rome, hoped he would take off at least some of the pressure of the situation he was in. All of those involved in passing the *lex Manilia* come across as selfish and irresponsible. They were prepared to change the command in what Dio describes as a largely successful war against a dangerous and resourceful enemy simply because they themselves hoped to benefit if Pompey was given the war against Mithridates. Whether the change of command was appropriate or not is here beside the point; what matters is how Dio portrays Rome's political elite as highly irresponsible, and the system as deeply dysfunctional. Once again, essentially all political decisions that were being made were carried out with ulterior motives.[14]

Another aspect of Roman politics Dio tries to show his readers is how the republican form of government encouraged a political culture where members of the political elite watched over one another trying to prevent any of their peers from becoming too popular, rich or powerful. One example of an attempt to take the wind out of a successful general's sails dates to the end of 62 when Pompey returned from the campaign against Mithridates and the ensuing settlement of the Near East. The campaign was arguably one of the most astonishing military achievements carried out by any Roman general to date. The relationship between Pompey and the Senate was hateful. A considerable share of the senators were still frustrated and jealous of how Pompey had won an extraordinary victory, and that he had used the tribunes and the *comitia tributa* to pass laws that offered him the commands in the first place, but also that he had pushed Lucullus and other senators out of the way to secure the command. With Pompey on his way back to Rome, the Senate feared a return similar to Sulla's and wondered whether Pompey would march on the capital and become the new dictator. To soften the victorious general, the Senate acknowledged the victory and voted Pompey the right to triumph, apparently before he reached the shores of Italy. To return the Senate's gesture, Pompey dissolved his army upon his arrival in Brundisium before he continued to Rome to receive a glorious celebration of his victory.

One of the issues that had to be negotiated was the reward of land to Pompey's soldiers, which in Late Republican Rome continued at the top of the political agenda. But before the question of land could be solved, Pompey's acts in the East had to be approved by the Senate who usually debated and then voted on all the acts in one packet. In his account of the moment when the acts were on the agenda, Dio offers another example of how for all the wrong reasons an envious and irresponsible Senate failed to ratify Pompey's activities in the east. As usual, Dio is merciless in his description of a dysfunctional political elite whose short-sightedness had the potential for a new civil war.

> At this time Pompey entered Italy and had Lucius Afranius and Metellus Celer appointed consuls, vainly hoping to achieve whatever he desired through them. He wished in particular to have some land given to his fellow-soldiers and to have all his acts confirmed, but he failed in these wishes at that time. For the optimates who even before this had not been pleased with him prevented votes being held on these questions. And as for the consuls themselves, Afranius, who knew how to dance better than to transact any business, was of no help to him at all, and Metellus, angry that Pompey had divorced his sister although he had children by her, completely opposed him in everything. And Lucius Lucullus, whom Pompey had once treated with contempt when he met him in Galatia, was very bitter against him, ordering him to return an account individually and separately of everything that he had done instead of asking for the approval of all his acts at once.
>
> Dio 37.49.1–4

In the following passages, Dio moves on to describe how Pompey was forced to give up, and he blames the situation on Metellus who Pompey openly accused of being jealous. But Dio also says that Pompey realized that he was not as powerful or influential as he thought he would be after the campaign in the East. Leaving a defeated Pompey behind, Dio moved on to Caesar, who is described as overly ambitious and heavily devoted to winning supreme power. The readers are given a reasonably detailed account of what happened in Rome after his return from Spain. Dio describes how the ambitious Caesar had his eyes fixed on the consulate but felt he needed support from some of Rome's most influential men. Consequently, he turned towards Pompey and Crassus, Rome's richest man and Pompey's opponent since the 70s, and managed to reconcile them by offering them a political alliance that would allow the three of them to dominate Roman politics in the years to come.

Dio describes in detail how Caesar felt no particular compassion for the two but he ruthlessly calculated that the three of them together would have the power to reach their own individual goals and the alliance would fall out to his advantage. Dio offers reasons for why Pompey and Crassus chose to step into the alliance. Once again, it was the fear of being left behind that motivated the cooperation, and the focus is on what each of them hoped to gain personally from such an alliance.

> On his side, Pompey was not as strong as he had hoped to be, and when he saw that Crassus was in power and that Caesar's influence was growing, he feared that he would be completely overthrown by them; and he hoped that if he let them share in his present advantages, he would win back his former authority through them. Crassus thought he ought to surpass everyone by reason of his family and his wealth; and since he was inferior by far to Pompey and thought that Caesar was going to rise to great heights, he wanted to set them in opposition to each other, in order that neither of them would prevail.
> Dio 37.56.3–4

The entire discussion of the first triumvirate is part of a criticism of how members of the city's political elite were always looking to do what was in their own best interest to win or retain their position at the centre of Roman politics. But what is particularly interesting is how the Senate's attempt to weaken Pompey backfired, as it gave him a reason to form the alliance with Caesar and Crassus, which in effect was what allowed Caesar to become as strong as he did. In that sense, the old guard in the Senate came under an even stronger pressure that might not have been the case had they allowed Pompey to fulfil the promise of land that he made to his soldiers. Instead, they let Caesar in and allowed him to acquire first the consulship and the war in Gaul before he turned on Rome, won the civil war, and introduced himself as a new monarch who acted like a king and prevented the senators from fulfilling their ambitions.

In his coverage of the land reforms Caesar passes, Dio narrates how the newly elected consul did everything he could to include the Senate in the design of the law. Apparently, none of the senators found any fault with the law and even recognized the need to find a solution to the question of land. When the Senate failed to support the law, it was because it feared that the man behind the proposal would become too powerful if he was the one to find a solution to redistribute the land in a fair and civilized manner (Dio 37.1–2). When the law was being presented, the Senate tried to block the proposal by not voting in its favour. Caesar on his part responded by turning to the people, and with help from Pompey and Crassus he managed to secure the support of the public. On the day of the election, Dio describes how Marcus Bibulus, Caesar's fellow consul, tried to prevent the vote from taking place by announcing that the rest of the year was a sacred period, which meant that the people would no longer be able to assemble. Caesar carried through the vote and Bibulus was thrown down the stairs of the temple of Castor and Pollux when he tried to block the law. Dio's account of the reform adds another example to the description of how dysfunctional the political system was, just as it shows that men of power did not follow the rules if they were somehow in the way. In how Dio tells the story, political violence was once again the standard tool being used in a political climate where none of the constitutional mechanisms to block laws and initiative that would go against the interests of the state were respected any longer.

Dio recognized that a land reform was needed. Not only would such a law ease the pressure from a growing population in Rome and increase the productivity of abandoned fields across Italy, but it would also offer the poor an opportunity to make a living. When the Senate could not support such a law it was not because they did not see they needed to make these changes or because they found any formal faults with how the law was carried out. What troubled them was the fear that Caesar was looking to strengthen his own standing to get ahead and improve his future options, not because he was particularly interested in the question of land or wanted to ease the everyday living of Rome's poor.

Dio could have left the Senate in the role of envious self-serving members of an elite who would oppose every solution that would make any of their peers stand out as a champion of the people. But right after the account of how the Senate feared that Caesar proposed the law in the first place only to further improve his relationship with the people, Dio confirmed that this was precisely the reason why the consul drew up the law and that he included the Senate in the law only so that it would be difficult for them not to support the proposal when it was announced. In the way Dio chooses to tell the story of Caesar's consulship and the agrarian law, none of those involved come out in anything like a positive light. Caesar proposed the law so that he would earn the support of the people. The Senate failed to approve what was a much-needed bill out of fear that Caesar would become too popular should he manage to offer an improvement to the unfair distribution of Rome's resources, and the people broke the law when they prevented Bibulus from exercising his constitutional rights. The implicit conclusion Dio draws is straightforward: a democratic form of government was never going to work but would always encourage strong but unfruitful competition among members of the political elite. This would eventually lead to strife, unrest and even civil war if the state was resourceful enough to unleash that kind of force.[15]

This was precisely what happened on 9 August 48 when Caesar and Pompey, the latter now supported by the Senate who feared Caesar more than their former enemy, clashed at the battle of Pharsalus in central Greece. Caesar won but only after he had traumatized Rome's armies by asking them to fight their fellow soldiers in his unstoppable effort to win the supreme power. Where Dio says that Pompey wanted to be second to none, Caesar for his part wanted to be first of all (Dio 41.54.1). As we saw in Chapter 1, Dio believed Caesar's dictatorship, or monarchy as he called it, to be a step in the right direction. But as we shall see, the only way to ensure a more stable form of government was to establish a more formalized one-man rule, where all military and political power was handed over to a modest ruler whose responsibility it was to maintain inner peace, political stability and prosperity. In Dio's narrative, Octavian, Caesar's grandnephew and his son by adoption, was the only man at the time of the dictator's death who would be able to undertake such a task. But before he could replace democracy with the legitimate and enlightened monarchy he was given credit for, he had to fight one of the most brutal civil wars in the history of Rome.

Monarchy returns

Octavian Augustus is one of the key characters in the *Roman History* and he is both Dio's favourite and his example of the ideal emperor later monarchs would be wise to follow. He was one who ended the civil war and replaced democratic rule with a form of monarchy that liberated the Romans from the terror and violence that followed as a natural consequence of unlimited competition. His years in power as both triumvir and emperor occupy twelve of the eighty books. Those twelve are equally divided between the civil war years and the Principate, and offer the longest and most detailed narrative of the reign of Augustus. Accordingly, scholars have paid much attention to Dio's account of the reign of Augustus.[16] Dio was not trying to hide Octavian's role in the war nor somehow to minimize his part in the brutal struggle for supreme power. Furthermore, Dio maintains the historical importance of the years between the death of Caesar in

44 and the introduction fifteen years later of Rome's first monarchy since the age of the early kings. Octavian's prominent position in Dio's work is also underlined by the way he is the only figure to appear in the *Roman History* who receives a real introduction before his first appearance in the narrative, which differs from how everybody else appears directly in the narrative without any previous presentation.[17]

As we have already seen, the form of monarchical rule Augustus introduced is defined as Dio's ideal form of constitution. This section, therefore, is devoted to how our historian shaped the narrative so that his version of Augustus comes across. Octavian fought so vigorously, in Dio's narrative, to save Rome from political chaos and the terror of civil war; and as an absolute monarch he took it upon himself to rule, not to satisfy his own ambition for power, but to serve the Roman people, observing the mandate he obtained from the Senate and the assembly in return for his triumviral powers (Dio 53.11). The version Dio offers is easily found in the official version Augustus passes on in the *Res Gestae* and the claim of how he, as Caesar's young heir, gathered his own army and freed the city from the fractions (*RG* 1). The brutality and political cynicism Octavian demonstrated was not, as such, a problem for Dio. Octavian operated in a dangerous world, where extreme situations called for extreme measures. However, the war and Octavian's role in it remain issues he felt he needed to address. In this respect, it is interesting to note that in the portrait of Octavian, the young triumvir comes across as not in any way different from any other member of the political elite. Like Caesar, Pompey and Antony, Octavian aimed for supreme rule and was as determined as they were to win the war

As we shall see, Octavian treated his enemies with no less brutality than his fellow triumvirs and he readily formed an alliance with Caesar's murderers to get Antony out of the way so that he would be the one to represent his uncle's will in Rome. What made Octavian different from the other dynasts and the members of the coalition who were behind the murder of Caesar, was how, in the way Dio tells the story, he stepped on to the political scene to do what was right for the Romans: to punish his uncle's murderers and to re-instate a form of monarchical rule that had been introduced when Caesar became dictator for life.

To prevail, Octavian needed to win supreme power but it was not, so Dio assures us, his ambition to rule or to be first that urged him on. As we shall see from a number of the examples Dio offers, Augustus ruled in respect of the mandate he got from the Senate and the Roman people in the early 20s. He insisted that his powers were never to be made permanent but had to be renewed every five or ten years, and to make every effort to include the Senate in the decision-making process (Dio 52.13.1.). In the course of the twelve books, Dio offers his own version of Octavian/Augustus, one that is not ahistorical. Dio's Augustus is rooted in the sources he had access to, including Augustus' own writings, but he also used other sources as can be seen in the account of the atrocities at Perusia, where Dio offers a different and more critical version than the one we have from Appian who used Augustus' autobiography as his source (Dio 48.13.3–4 and App. *B Civ.* 5.48). What Dio does is to shape the account of Augustus so the new emperor fits the historian's own ideals of the kind of ruler Rome needed, which again underlines his potential as a leader figure that later emperors would be wise to mirror.

Dio's coverage of Augustus is modelled around three points of view: that the young triumvir had the right to fight the civil wars and that his acts in the course of the conflict were measured and necessary; that he obtained a clear mandate from Rome's political institutions to govern as a sole ruler; and that he had the right kind of character to rule in a fair and balanced manner. The version of how Octavian had an almost hereditary right to succeed Caesar is built upon a story of how the dictator left both his powers and his status as Rome's sole ruler to his young grandnephew. After the battle at Pharsalus where

Caesar defeated Pompey, Caesar received the title imperator for life, and the right to pass it on to his sons. In the passage, Dio emphasizes that it was the title of imperator together with the name Caesar that defined the imperial office. Later, Dio has Maecenas remind Octavian that he might want to consider using imperator as his formal title if he is unhappy with the term king (Dio 43.44.2–3 and 52.40.1–2).

In a third passage, Dio describes how, as Caesar learned about Octavian's many qualities, he wanted to leave the young man his power and position in the Roman society.

> Being childless and basing great hopes upon him [Octavian], Caesar loved and cherished him, intending to leave him as heir to his name, authority, and monarchy.
>
> Dio 45.1.2

Dio uses the term *monarchia* for Caesar's dictatorship. In the following passages, Dio offers no thoughts on how such transaction of powers should take place, nor does he discuss the legal complications that would be involved and, in the narrative, Octavian is not making any claim for Caesar's political power when at his arrival in Rome he asked to have his inheritance handed over. The notion that Caesar's powers were something the dictator was able to pass on to his adoptive son is an anachronism on Dio's part that relates to the imperial period, where it was normal that sons followed their fathers to the throne. Dio would have been well aware of this, but he gives Octavian the legally-binding right to step into Caesar's footsteps and fight the civil war to assume the position that Caesar, as the legitimate monarch, had passed onto him.

Having planted a seed in his readers' mind of how Octavian had a right to Caesar's sovereign position, Dio moves on to describe how Octavian had the necessary skills and the right nature to lead the Romans towards a better future. Even if he was young and unconventional, he was better at dealing with public affairs than any of the older men involved in Roman politics at the time (Dio 45.5.1–2). Octavian proved uncompromising in the civil war. He is said to have been less keen on the prescriptions than Antony and Lepidus were, a version that differs from the one offered by Suetonius in his biography of the divine Augustus, where Octavian is said to have been against proscription at first but no less firm than his allies when they were carried out (Dio 47.7.1–4 and Suet. *Aug.* 27.1). At Perusia, Octavian showed no sign of mercy when he defeated the city and the coalition of Roman nobles, and then burned everything, killed many residents and executed hundreds of Roman senators and *equites* (Dio 48.15.1–6).

In Dio's version of the civil wars, it was Octavian who pushed for war both against Antony and Sextus Pompeius, the son of Pompey the Great, who was defeated in 36 at Naulochus on the northern shores of Sicily.[18] Sextus had succeeded in offering enough opposition to the triumvirs to be included in the leadership and to become Antony's ally. But as the war between Octavian and Sextus moved closer, Antony withdrew his support for the young Pompeian because he needed more land troops to hold his position in the East in the wars against Parthia and Armenia. As Octavian was the only one he could turn to, Antony supplied the ships that allowed Octavian and Agrippa to fight and defeat Sextus (Dio 48.45–49; 49.11–16).

Octavian was also the one who pushed for war against Antony and Egypt when he used his enemy's testament to try and convince the Romans that Antony wanted to leave Rome to Cleopatra (Dio 50.3–4). Dio gives his readers the impression that Octavian was passing on rumours that were not entirely true. However, that does not change how Dio firmly believes that Octavian still had justice on his side. If we look at how Dio describes the civil war between 44 and 30, it soon becomes clear that the way in which Octavian differs from the other dynasts is that he wanted to do what was in the best interests of the Commonwealth, not because he wanted power. The means Octavian was prepared to use are largely the same, or even more cynical, than those implied by Caesar who did not proscribe any of his enemies but instead showed a great deal of clemency to those who had sided with Pompey.

As we saw in Chapter 1, Dio embraces the notion of a monarch with undivided powers, and he uses his narrative of the age of Augustus to demonstrate that Rome's first emperor was the one who organized a form of government where the Senate was let back into the decision-making process. Another important point Dio wants to make is how it was Augustus who took the necessary steps to introduce the kind of rule Dio saw as the best possible way to rule Rome. To get his message across, Dio offers an account of how, as a result of the senators' declining interests in the political process, Augustus made arrangements that would force or encourage senators to attend meetings. New meetings were scheduled well in advance on days where no other business took place, notice had to be given if a senator was absent and fines had to be paid if senators did not have a legitimate reason not to attend meetings (Dio 55.3.1–4). To make politics worthwhile for members of the Senate and encourage them to take on the role as the emperors' advisors, Augustus set up boards where the senators could read about new laws and proposals before the meeting so that they could be prepared and offer Augustus an informed opinion (Dio 55.4; 55.34.1).[19]

In that sense, Dio's Augustus saved Rome by ending the civil war and by introducing a more stable form of government where he had both the power and the responsibility to rule as an absolute ruler but also the insight to include the experience and advice of the senators, who, under his guidance, were slowly finding their way into the role as the emperor's loyal advisors. In his conclusion on the reign of Augustus, Dio praises the monarchy that Rome's first emperor introduced and makes it clear that in the eyes of the subjects, Augustus was to be recognized as someone who had done what was necessary. In other words, at the death of Augustus, the Romans had finally come to the conclusion that by stepping in at a critical moment after Caesar's murder and by taking the task of monarchical rule on his own shoulders, Augustus had freed the Romans from the slavery of the factions that the continuous struggle for superiority and supremacy brought on the city and its inhabitants. The real challenge was to uphold the principles that Augustus introduced: modesty, cooperation and mutual respect between the emperor and the empire's elite, something Dio is moving on to show in his books on Imperial Rome that was more easily said than done, and a form of government where the monarch was more concerned about the needs of the Commonwealth than he was about the glory, pomp and shallow honorific titles that came with being emperor.

The ideal emperor

In his books on Imperial Rome, one of Dio's aims was to demonstrate to the reader what good government was about. In short, Dio believed that the best form of government was one where the emperor tried to imitate Augustus and the form of rule he introduced during the 44 years he was in power as sole ruler. This implied a genuine desire to include the Senate in the decision-making process, a commitment to honour Rome's laws, ensure fair trials and a strong commitment to not accommodate political motivated prosecutions, as well as a devotion to the task of ruling the Romans and their empire in a qualified and serious manner.

It is particularly interesting to note that in Dio's eyes, in a text that emphasizes how a monarchical form of constitution is to be preferred at all costs, most emperors never found the balance between an inclusive and legitimate form of government and the right to rule in absolute terms. Instead, what most of them practised was a form of rule where in one way or another they bypassed the Senate and ignored the advice from what in Dio's mind were men of experience and already proven political and military records. As a result, many emperors chose a despotic form of government, where instead of engaging with the Senate, they saw its members as an opposition or a threat they needed to suppress.

Similar to Tacitus in the *Annals* and Suetonius in his biographies of the twelve Caesars from Julius Caesar to Domitian, Dio is a critic of the Julio-Claudian dynasty. The emperor Tiberius, Augustus's successor, is criticized for his dishonest and manipulative nature, where he tried to have the senators expose themselves by never revealing what he thought about certain people or of the matters he discussed in the Senate (Dio 57.1.1–6 and Tac. *Ann.* 1.11). At first, Tiberius rejected rumours and abstained from mock trials, but he changed his course after the death of Germanicus when he felt more secure on the throne (Dio 57.18–19 and Suet. *Tib.* 59–62).

The next emperor in line, young Caligula, is described, and probably rightly so, as a tyrant who humiliated the Senate and terrorized the senators by prosecuting innocent members of the political elite. Caligula was young and inexperienced with no political career or first-hand knowledge of the Senate or the army. He was eccentric and keen on gladiatorial games and spent vast sums of money on his lavish lifestyle (Dio 57.10.7; 59.22.3–4, and Suet. *Cal.* 38.1–4). Claudius, on the other hand, was a capable administrator and a successful general but he turned to the assistance of his freemen, leaving the senators on the side-line (Dio 60.2.4. See also Suet. Clau. 25.5 and Tac. *Ann.* 11.33.1; 11.35.1). Nero was perhaps the worst of all the Julio-Claudian emperors. He had no real interest in governing the empire and when he finally committed himself somewhat to the task, he tried to outdo Caligula in brutality (Dio 61.4–5. On the death of Claudius' biological son Britannicus, see Tac. *Ann.* 8.17, and Suet. *Ner.* 7.1). What the Julio-Claudian emperors had in common was how they all came to power through dynastic succession, not because of their qualifications but because they were the emperor's son or male relative. Tiberius had the experience from politics and his career in the army but lacked the necessary people skills to rule in a fair and balanced manner, and Claudius, for his part, was hard-working and successful but sidestepped the Senate when he chose to rely on his slaves and freemen.

The first emperor in Dio's narrative who met Dio's ideals of good government was Vespasian, a man of experience with considerable military credentials as the commander of the Syrian army, and someone who had followed the traditional way up through the political hierarchy. It is in this mixture of experience, modesty and a determination to bring the senators back into the decision-making process that Dio sees the qualities of Vespasian and therefore as the definition of the ideal monarch.

In the course of what is admittedly a short portrait of the emperor, we hear of how Vespasian asked the senators for advice on every matter, how he attended the Senate meetings and comported himself as if he were still one of the senators. Dio emphasizes how the emperor did not kill any senator undeservedly, which is some achievement considering that he came to power after a civil war (Dio 65.10). Other emperors that fell into the same category of the ideal emperor were Nerva, who also took advice from his fellow senators (Dio 68.1–2) and Trajan, who, for his part, is praised for not having killed innocent men and for never having suffered from jealousy. Dio also offers a description of Trajan's physique, where he notes how the emperor, at the age of 42, was at his prime both physically and mentally (Dio 68.6.3). The emperor was not reckless as a young man or careless as an older man, a remark that may be read as another reminder of how the ideal emperor was a man of age and experience, who was no longer impulsive but still fully committed to doing the job as well as possible.

According to Dio, when it went wrong and monarchical rule turned into tyranny it was because the emperors did not live up to the responsibility of ruling as absolute monarchs in respect and in cooperation with the senators, taking their advice but at the same time making sure that any competition for the prestigious posts and military commands remained a thing of the past. A stable government and inner peace would always be the responsibility of the emperor who, Dio believed, was to dedicate himself fully to the task of governing the empire, taking care of people's needs but without buying them off and maintaining strong discipline in the army. Where emperors such as Vespasian, Trajan and Hadrian managed to meet these obligations, other less experienced men such as Caligula, Nero, Commodus and Caracalla failed because they did not care much for the work behind the title, or because they did not listen to the Senate and failed to benefit from their expertise.

In Dio's eyes, greed and personal ambitions continued as an integral part of Roman politics and war between Roman armies. Ambitious pretenders to the throne continued to traumatize people across the empire and the armies. Dio illustrates the point by drawing the reader's attention to the battle between Vitellius and Vespasian in 69, and how difficult it was for the soldiers to fight and kill their comrades (Dio 64.13), and how, at a horse race in Rome, they protested against the war Septimius Severus fought against Albinus (Dio 76.[75].4.11–12). What had changed for the better was how competition to win the people's vote was no longer a part of Roman politics and, more importantly, that the army was now in the hands of one man whose responsibility it was to command all the soldiers and appoint his own generals. The risk of war between a commander in one of the provinces and the emperor was therefore drastically reduced, even if civil war would still show its ugly face from time to time.

This was mostly the case when the death of an emperor left a void to be filled, such as after the death of Nero or in the chaos following the murder of Pertinax. In moments like these, Rome's generals had to decide whether they would try to take the power themselves or back one of the other pretenders to the throne. Dio describes such troubled times when he points to the death of Pertinax and the auction for the throne that Didius Julianus won. The struggle between Severus and Niger shows how fragile Roman politics was, particularly if no obvious successor was in place at the death of the emperor in power. The solution Dio offers was not the reintroduction of dynastic rule that Septimius Severus was looking for but the system where the next emperor in line was chosen and adopted from among the most capable members of the Senate.

Dio offers in his books on Imperial Rome a very personal view, and even if he shared his thoughts with other contemporary men of letters, he still offers an account of Imperial Rome that supports his own ideas of how monarchy was the only form of government to ensure stability for any state, but particularly one as strong and resourceful as Rome. This tendentious approach to the history of Rome is not without difficulties when what Dio has to say about episodes, individuals and certain periods of time is used to reconstruct Roman political history. How we are to approach Dio's text and the analysis he offers is the theme in the following chapter, which is also devoted to what it is Dio does well.

3

Cassius Dio and His History of Rome

After his return to Bithynia and his home in Nicaea, Dio might well have spent most of his last years finishing his *Roman History*. His death has traditionally been set at some time in the mid-230s but there is no way of being sure. What we can say, however, is that Xiphilinus seems to have found nothing about Alexander Severus' later years in power in Dio's last book. Instead, his Roman history ends with the historian leaving the capital and the world of Roman politics behind. Who read Dio and how many of his readers were in the mid-third- and fourth-century Roman Empire is difficult to tell, just as it is difficult to establish what kind of impact Dio's thoughts on Roman politics and history more broadly had on members of the political elite in Rome and across the empire. However, various studies have suggested with confidence that Dio was read by contemporary and later historians.[1]

As is the case for most other ancient writers, we have no way of knowing whether he published some of the books as he finished them or whether he waited until all eighty books were completed. It is worth remembering that Dio delivered a harsh critique of the Severan dynasty, which, even if we should not exaggerate the danger of expressing criticism, could have posed a threat, particularly if his criticism of Septimius Severus was made public when Caracalla was still emperor. What he may have done is discuss his thoughts about politics and different emperors with friends and trusted senators, who would have shared his historical interests or his frustrations over the contemporary political situation. To gain views on the text he was writing, Dio may have invited people to his house in Rome or to his villa in Campania, where he would have read out part of his books or sections he had recently finished, just as the Roman senator Pliny the Younger tells us he did when he finished the written version of his speech to Trajan as a thank you note for having received the consulship (Plin. *Ep.* 3.18). Similarly, Dio may have distributed copies of some of his books as he finished them, and they may have been available in libraries in Rome or outside the capital, or in the houses of some of his friends.

Most of the early books on Republican Rome and the early empire would probably not have caused any concern at the court of Caracalla or the late emperors. It is also worth remembering that until he published the last six books of the *Roman History*, Dio would have been known as a writer who wrote favourably about dreams that predicted Septimius Severus' accession to power and of his role in the civil war with Niger and Albinus. If Dio began working on *Roman History* some time after the civil wars, he would have written a large part of the book in the mid-220s when he served as governor in Africa, Dalmatia and Pannonia, which again would mean that his options were limited had he wanted to reach a Roman readership.

There is much to suggest that Dio was read as a source both by contemporary historians, such as Herodian from Syria and by later ancient writers, such as the fourth-century author of the *Historia Augusta* who wrote his controversial biographies of the emperors of the second and third centuries. However, Dio is not mentioned explicitly by either of the two writers and there is no clear-cut example of how his text or points of views were redeployed. This has led to some debate about his importance as a source for later authors in antiquity. A reasonable approach to the question is to assume that Dio was read in full or in part by Herodian and the author of the *Historia Augusta*, but that we should not expect either of them to have incorporated the *Roman History* into their text.[2]

In the age of emperor Justinian (527–565), a number of authors of authors, such as John the Lydian and Peter the Patrician, turned to

Dio and his thoughts on monarchical rule in an attempt to offer alternative solutions to the emperor's belief in absolute monarchy. Dio's coverage of Roman politics and his thoughts about the reign of Augustus and the imperial period were brought into a current constitutional debate at the court at Constantinople as an authority on political thought. One example of how Dio was used in the constitutional debate is when John the Lydian quotes him directly in the *De Magistratibus,* to support his claim that even Romulus behaved tyrannically (*Mag.* 1.7.3). As we saw at the beginning of Chapter 2, Dio agreed that most of the kings in the Regal Period were tyrants who ruled without the support of the political elite and were therefore not legitimate monarchs who governed with respect for the mandate they had received.[3]

Apart from a reasonably detailed explanation of how the Principate was organized, Dio would also have offered later readers a rather personal take on Roman politics, and how greed, unregulated competition and self-serving interests continued to torment Roman history from the moment the city was founded. They would also find thorough analyses of why a monarchical form of government was what Rome needed, and equally long discussions of what kind of monarchy, or monarch, would ensure the most stable form of rule. As we have seen, many of Dio's thoughts on what constituted an ideal rule, or how greed and envy polluted the political climate, were available in the writings of other authors such as Sallust, Velleius Paterculus, Tacitus and in the *Panegyricus* of Pliny the Younger, even if they were less fully argued or supported with fewer examples. However, what Dio offered was a relatively long narrative that covered more than 1,000 years of Rome's political history from the Regal Period to right before the 'Barrack' Emperors changed Roman politics forever in the mid-third century. After the 230s, the city of Rome gradually lost its status as the unchallenged centre of the empire, and the senatorial order was no longer able to secure its privileged position as commanders in the army or as governors in the provinces where the army was stationed. This was a change that Dio was very aware of and partly the reason why he was so attentive to the role that the Senate should be given as the emperors' advisory board and as the pool of talent from which the current emperor should draw his successor.

Seen as a whole, what would have interested authors such as John the Lydian and Peter the Patrician the most is likely to have been his thoughts on the good monarch and how he was to respect his peers by respecting their views in his decisions. Dio's ideal emperor held absolute power but he would soon earn the label of a tyrant if he ignored the advice his former peers offered him. Instead, as Dio saw it, the monarch was to honour and uphold a system of exchange, where the political elite accepted a considerable loss of political liberty in exchange not just for peace and stability, but for the right to be heard and give advice as a political authority with roots in every part of the empire. In sixth-century Constantinople, magistrates, members of the political establishment, philosophers and other men of letters saw the world of politics in much the same light as Dio and responded to emperor Justinian absolutist approach in a similar fashion to how Dio had to the reign of Septimius Severus three centuries earlier.

What Dio also offers his ancient and more modern readers is both a descriptive account of how and why Roman politics changed in the way it did, and a narrative that would provide them with an analytic account of the history of Rome from the foundation of the city to the age of the Severan emperors. Judging from the excerpts from Xiphilinus, one of the answers Dio gives is that part of the instability of his own age was the result of Septimius Severus' decision to rest his powers on the support of soldiers rather than on his peers in the Senate. Dio describes how Severus passed the advice to his sons that they should first and foremost make sure to meet the needs of the soldiers, which meant that they were to pay them well before they took care of anyone else (Dio 77[76].15.2). Similar stories are told in the coverage of Caracalla who was just as keen to accommodate the needs of his soldiers and ensure that they knew that they were more important and valuable to him than the senators (Dio 78[77].9-10).

Another point Dio made was how uncertain the political climate was in Rome after the death of Marcus Aurelius, where every emperor except Septimius Severus died a violent death and the relationship between the Senate and the court went from respectful and reasonably cooperative to hostile and threatening. In Dio's own words, with the accession of Commodus an age of gold was replaced by one of iron and rust, a vivid image that sets the tone for the following description of how Commodus and all the later emperors, except Pertinax, used terror and humiliation as political tools to suppress the Senate (Dio 72[71].36.4). In Dio's account of his own years in politics, Commodus was keener on animal hunts and gladiatorial combats than he was on running the empire (Dio 73[72].1-4 and 73[72].17-18). Caracalla had a similar interest in gladiatorial shows and horse races, and showed a condescending attitude towards the senators where he, according to Dio, left them standing outside his quarters most of the day while he entertained himself as a gladiator (Dio 78[77].17.3-4). Elagabal took the liberty to introduce a new Syrian deity with the same name and raise this new god above Jupiter in the Roman pantheon (Dio 80.11-12).

What Dio describes is a climate of fear and uncertainty. Commodus issued a direct threat when he held up the head of the ostrich he had just killed (Dio 73[72].21.1). Dio tries to make light of the entire episode, which he makes out to be more ridiculous than intimidating. Other episodes were surely more disturbing to the historian, such as when Didius Julianus brought the Praetorian Guard with him into the Senate at the time he was announced as the new emperor, or when on his return from the war against Albinus, Septimius Severus came into the Senate and threatened its members while offering praise to Sulla, Marius and Augustus for their cruelty (Dio 74[73].12.6). Another example from the reign of Severus that shook Dio to the core is set in a Senate meeting where an investigation against Popilius Pedo Apronianus, the governor of Asia at the time, was conducted because his nurse had dreamed that Apronianus would one day become emperor. During the procedure, a bald-headed senator is said to have heard about the nurse's dream, which according to Dio made every thin-haired senator fear for his life. The historian describes a desperate situation to his readers.

> When we heard this, we were in a terrible position; for neither had that man said nor had Severus written anyone's name, but such was the distress that even those who had never visited the house of Apronianus, and not only the bald-headed but even those who were bald on their forehead, were afraid. And no one was confident, except those who had unusually heavy hair, but all of us looked round at such men, and there was a murmur: 'It's So-and so.' 'No, it's So-and so.' I will not hide what happened to me then, even if it is totally ridiculous. For I was so gripped with helplessness that I actually felt with my hand for the hair on my head. And many others had the same experience. And we looked to those who were more or less bald, to transfer our own danger to them; until it was read out that the bald-headed man had worn a purple-bordered toga.
>
> Dio 77[76].8.3–5

Dio moves on to describe how Baebius Marcellinus was picked out and prosecuted, and how, outside the Senate house, he said goodbye to his children, telling them that the only thing he regretted was that he would have to leave them behind alive.

Whether Herodian and the writer of *Historia Augusta* read about the terror of political instability in Dio's books or in another contemporary source, there are traces in their writing of how the political elite in third-century Rome were traumatized. But it is interesting to note that unlike the author of *Historia Augusta* and Dio, who relied on his own experience from living in Rome, Herodian's ambition was to write the history of the Severans based on a variety of sources and facts, and to offer a more comprehensible narrative of why the climate between the Senate and Severus turned from initially positive to hostile and suspicious. The atmosphere was still hostile and the emperors were still brutal but we get a better idea of why Severus may have acted in the way he did on his return from war against Albinus. Albinus fought with support from members of the Senate not to defend himself, but to push Severus out of the way. In Dio's version, it was Severus who no longer had any need for Albinus after Niger had fallen. This made the emperor take the necessary steps to remove his previous and ambitious ally and, something Dio is not telling us, to make room for his sons' entrance in the government.

This lack of attention to detail or calculated attempt to steer the reader in a certain direction is part of the reason why modern scholars have questioned the information Dio offers about his own contemporary years. One concern is that Dio's coverage of the Severan years is too influenced by his own, mostly negative experiences with the emperors to offer a balanced account of the reign. In addition, another point that modern scholars have raised is that Dio's reservations about essentially all the emperors he experienced first-hand, drove him towards an overly positive portrait of Augustus. As a result, scholars have questioned whether, when writing the history of Augustan Rome, Dio was commenting implicitly on the reign of his own contemporary emperors.

Another point of criticism was offered by Millar – how Dio failed to recognize the importance of Christianity and the mass migration of tribes into the Roman Empire that slowly began in the late-second century but took on more dramatically from the third century onwards. Where the one-sided approach to the Severan emperors represents a methodological issue that needs to be taken into consideration, thoughts about how Dio could have been more aware of challenges from Christian groups or from pressure in the borders are less obvious.[4]

Christianity and the pressure from migration have no place in the books on the High Empire, and even if migration clearly was not important to Dio, it should be remembered that very little of what he wrote about Marcus Aurelius has been preserved in Xiphilinus' excerpts. Given the favourable portrait Dio offers in what is left of his coverage of the emperor, it is to be expected that the historian would have had something to add on the wars Aurelius fought against Marcomannic or Sarmatic tribes. It was surely part of the emperor's own self-representation, as demonstrated by the column that was set up to celebrate the victory that was on people's minds in Rome at the time Dio was living in the capital.

On the other hand, it also has to be remembered that Dio's primary focus was devoted to the struggle for power between members of the political elite in Rome. When Dio moves his focus out of the city, it is to cover conflicts or events that relate to politics in the capital or to conflicts between members of the political elite in Rome. As a descendant from one of the distinguished families in second-century Nicaea, Dio has surprisingly little to offer on life in the provinces or on how Roman power was perceived from a provincial point of view. This may be seen as a limitation on his value as a source of Roman history in general, but we should recall that he was not trying to cover all aspects of the history of the Roman Empire and should be read on his own premise: as a historian predominantly interested in Roman politics at its highest level and in constitutional history.

As we shall see in the following, Dio offers a number of coherent, well informed and indispensable analyses of Roman politics that help us to understand episodes or the motives of those involved, which, again, would have been obscure if we did not have his contribution. However, not surprisingly, there are parts of the narrative and aspects of his approach to Roman politics and history more broadly that offer considerable problems if used as a source to reconstruct how certain situations unfolded or why members of the political elite and emperors acted in the way they did.

Part of the reason why from time to time Dio is less credible as a source ties into his primary focus on the competition for power and to his strong bias against democracy. This preconception against political liberty made Dio look very one-sidedly at the flaws and failings in the political system that he felt was incapable as a form of government. Other challenges are the many examples of unsubtle coverage of the admittedly stressful reign of the emperors of his time, which fails to provide balanced versions of, for instance, why the civil war between Albinus and Severus broke out or why Severus lost faith in the senators and turned towards his soldiers instead.

Dio's history of Rome

Apart from the claim that no one in Republican Rome took part in politics to serve in the best interests of the state, the strong criticism of essentially all the emperors in Dio's own lifetime and the overall positive approach to the reign of Augustus represent significant methodological issues when the text is used as a source on Augustan Rome. However, as we shall see, the detailed account of Octavian's route to power and the arrangement of the mandate he received after winning the civil war make the *Roman History* a fascinating read and an indispensable source not just for the reign of Augustus but also more generally for the organization of Roman politics in the early imperial period.

The description of how a modest and respectful Augustus made his best efforts to include the Senate in the decision-making process stands out as an antithesis to the many later emperors who paid less attention to senatorial opinion and well-being. The description of how Augustus encouraged the senators to attend Senate meetings and participate in the decision-making process by offering advice on new laws stands in contrast to Severus' threats and unfounded prosecutions of the members of the political elite. It is, therefore, with sound reason that modern scholars have raised concerns about whether Dio is offering a reliable account of the reign of Augustus or using Rome's first emperor as an ideal of good government as a way to criticize how Septimius Severus suddenly alienated the senators.

One example where Dio's version of the moderate Augustus is particularly misleading is found in the different approach to the honorary decrees that Julius Caesar and Octavian received after they won the civil wars against Pompey and Antony respectively. In the account of how Julius Caesar was partly responsible for his own death, Dio points out that the extraordinary honours he received after the war against Pompey undermined the dictator's chances to rule because he was elevated above the rest of what he already knew to be an envious and hateful group of ambitious senators. When Caesar was not consistently clear in his rejection of the kingship, he made himself vulnerable to the elite who were all in politics to gain as much power and prestige for themselves as possible. Dio criticizes Caesar's lack of modesty and how he accepted honours that he thought he deserved (Dio 44.3.1–3). The comment on Caesar's inability to decline what Dio sees as largely empty titles and honorary decrees, ties into the description of how Caesar had always wanted to supersede everyone in Rome but also to the larger narrative the *Roman History* of how most men in Roman politics lacked the art of moderation.

In his coverage of the honours Octavian received after his victory against Antony and Egypt at Actium and in Alexandria, Dio offers no criticism at all of how the victorious triumvir was celebrated. The honours that were voted to Octavian were no less spectacular than the ones received by Caesar, and some of them, such as the libation that was to be poured in honour of Octavian at both private and public dinners, the admission of his name to the hymn of the Salii (a song where Rome's gods are named) and the sacrifice performed by one of the consuls when the triumvir returned to Rome, had clear divine connotations (Dio 51.19). Without questioning whether Octavian deserved these honours, Dio mentions how Rome's new sole ruler asked that the decision to have the people come out and greet him at his return to Rome was not put into effect. By showing what could then be perceived as a more modest victory, Dio bypasses the issue of whether the honours were appropriate or not, or whether Octavian should have taken the opportunity to decline some of the more extravagant honours, such as those that tied him to the sphere of the gods.

The coverage of the honours voted to Octavian when he was still on his way back to Rome allow us to see in what way Dio works as a historian. One of his prime concerns was to tell what he knew about Roman history and the political situation, including the honours voted to the victorious Octavian. These were details Dio would have read about either in the Senate archives or in the writing of other historians. It is interesting to see how he was not applying the same standards to Octavian as he was to Caesar. Where the latter was greedy, insensitive and wrong to have accepted honours that would elevate him above his peers, Octavian is never questioned. Instead, Dio upholds the tale of a ruler who took power into his own hands because it was required of him, but at the same time, Dio wants us to believe, as someone who made sure that he would not elevate himself above his peers.

The modesty of Augustus is particularly apparent in the account of how he received the cult in Pergamum when the triumvir was on his way back from Egypt in the winter between 30 and 29. This passage contains the only written testimony for how worship of Augustus was first introduced.

> Meanwhile, besides attending to the general business, Caesar (Octavian), granted permission for the dedication of sacred areas in Ephesus and in Nicaea to Rome and to Caesar, his father, whom

> he named the hero Julius. At that time, these cities had achieved pre-eminence in Asia and in Bithynia respectively. He instructed the Romans resident in these cities to honour these two divinities; but he permitted the non-Romans, whom he styled Hellenes, to consecrate areas to himself, the Asians to have theirs in Pergamum and the Bithynians theirs in Nicomedia. Beginning under him, this practice, has continued under other emperors, not only in the case of the Hellenic nations but also in that of all the others, in so far as they are subject to the Romans. For in the capital itself and in the rest of Italy, nobody, however worthy of renown he has been, has dared to do this; still, even their various divine honours are granted after their death upon such emperors as have ruled justly, and, in fact, shrines are built to them.
>
> Dio 51.20.6–8

We now know that Dio is mistaken or deliberately misleading when he claims no emperor ever received worship on the Italian peninsula. There were cults to Augustus in Italian cities from as early as the year 15 BCE, four years after the temple to the goddess Roma and Augustus was inaugurated in Pergamum. Another problem with what Dio writes about the early cults to Augustus and Julius Caesar is that there are no other references to the Caesar and Roma cults that he claims were consecrated in Ephesus and Nicaea. The lack of any sources that corroborate Dio's claim that two cults were inaugurated in Asia and Bithynia seriously questions the distinction the historian draws between the cults to the living and the deceased emperors.[5]

As shown by the epigraphic material from the cities, Roman citizenships of local origin served as priests in cults to the living Augustus from as early as final decades BCE. When compared to the material from Italy that shows that Roman citizens in Italy also worshipped Augustus right from the moment when the cities in Asia Minor consecrated similar cults, there is every reason to assume that Dio is being deliberately manipulative. As a strong critic of emperor-worship, and as an author whose objective it was to show how at least part of

Augustus' success was his modesty and sensitivity to the Senate's need for respect, Dio was compelled to downplay the extraordinary honours and the worship that were consecrated in honour of the emperor.

Another concern is the conclusion Dio draws about the reign of Augustus in book 56. Here the reader is presented with Dio's own thoughts about how at Augustus' death it was widely recognized that Rome's first emperor had freed the Romans from the terror of political instability caused by individual ambitions, and from the struggle for power between members of the political elite. According to Dio, it was widely acknowledged that in order to win the civil war and provide a more stable form of government, Augustus was forced to use extreme measures during the civil war (Dio 56.43.4). Over the following passages, where the violent introduction of monarchical rule is justified, Augustus is freed from guilt and the accusation that he used unnecessary force to acquire supreme power. Dio may be seen here to oppose the view of how Rome's first monarch since the Regal Period was a tyrant who wanted absolute power at any cost. Tacitus paints a very different picture in his *Annals*, where Augustus not only fought a brutal civil war to remove his immediate opponents, men such as Sextus Pompeius and Antony, but also the opposition, from what was left of the Senate. Here the members were either too afraid or too comfortable to oppose the regime and therefore happy or ready to settle with the status their seats in the Senate offered them (Tac. *Ann.* 1.1–10).

It is beyond reasonable doubt that Dio read Tacitus but also that he strongly disagreed with how his older peer chose to paint the picture of the man who ended not just the civil wars but also put a stop to political freedom and the competition that laid the ground for war and strife between citizens. One reason why Tacitus and Dio saw Augustus so differently is of course that Augustus was Dio's ideal emperor. Dio would, therefore, have to defend his favourite kind of monarch against some of the criticism of Augustus that Tacitus might have levelled. Another reason why Dio spoke so favourably of

Augustus could also be that the latter actually did work hard to establish a form of monarchy where it was the intention to offer the Senate a meaningful role in the political process as Dio claimed Augustus made an effort to ensure happened.

In order to prove his point, Dio refers to a general opinion among members of the political elite at the time that Augustus had done well and that they, in his absence, now realized that they were going to miss him greatly (Dio 56.43.4). Extreme times called for extreme measures, and Dio moves on to assure his readers that the Romans understood that Augustus had to be firm to introduce a form of government where political freedom was exchanged for peace and stability. Even if Dio is right in his claim that Augustus was to be excused for the way he acted in the civil war, it is still troubling how he refers to a common opinion that fits perfectly with his own heavily idealized view of Augustus, monarchy and the flaws of democracy.

The importance of Dio's historical analysis

We are trained to pay attention to flaws and failings in texts and in argumentation. Dio's *Roman History* is unevenly written, a point which sometimes adds to the impression that he is not always in full control of his material or that he is not offering the most plausible account of the events and motives he describes. In the rest of this chapter, I will try to show how the strengths of the *Roman History* outweighed its shortcomings. Paradoxically, the focus on the failings of democracy is also what makes the text an indispensable source for Roman history. Its biased attitude towards democracy aside, the coherent account of more than a millennium makes it an unusual work of Roman history. Dio's focus on the greed, envy, immodesty and ultimate failure of the political elite, represents the same kind of thinking and the same conclusion as those offered by many modern historians for whom the political crisis in Late Republican Rome was one without alternative.[6]

The one-sided approach to politics in Republican Rome causes concern, and we may disagree with the many generalizing assumptions of how, for instance, only Cato took a genuine interest in the Commonwealth. Also, the consistently negative account of the fall of Republican Rome and the catastrophe of democracy represents a form of political realism that Dio ended up overstating in an attempt to prove his point. However, what Dio offers is still a series of examples that demonstrate how greed, envy and short-termism dominated Roman politics throughout the 1,000 years he covers. An example of an episode where the coverage is credible for the most part is the account of what happened at Perusia in the winter of 41 to 40, when Octavian starved the city to surrender.

The Battle of Perusia grew out of an attempt to settle some of Julius Caesar's veterans who had fought Marcus Junius Brutus and Gaius Cassius Longinus, two of the leading senators in the plot against Caesar, together with Octavian and Mark Antony at the Battle of Philippi in 42. After he had led the triumvirs to victory against Caesar's murderers, Antony took possession over the East to follow up on Caesar's plans to conquer Parthia (modern Iran and the successor to the Persian kingdom). Octavian, for his part, returned to Italy where it was his task to settle the soldiers in cities that had already been singled out after the people had granted the triumvirs a mandate to restore the state.

The confiscation of the land and the settlement of the veterans into the civic communities was met with considerable opposition. The veterans assumed more land than they had been allotted, members of the civic elites tried to resist the confiscations, Sextus Pompeius threatened the supply of corn to Rome, and Antony's younger brother Lucius Antonius and wife Fulvia did what they could to complicate the settlement further by leading an armed resistance against the young triumvir.

When the two parties met at Perusia, Lucius Antonius and his followers took hold of the city before they had to surrender as he realized that the reinforcements they were hoping for were not coming to their rescue. What happened after the surrender is not entirely clear and ancient sources offer at least two different versions, one by Dio and one by Appian (App. *B Civ* 5.48.1 and Dio 48.14.3–5). In Dio's account of events, Octavian orders the execution of the political elite in Perusia, including hundreds of Roman senators and *equites* at the altar to Julius Caesar. In Appian's account of what happened, Octavian ordered that his own friends and some of the centurions were to make sure that the Roman nobles were treated with respect. Dio unveils a brutal affair.

> The leader (Lucius Antonius) and some others obtained pardon, but most of the senators and knights were put to death. And the story is that they did not suffer death in a simple manner, but were led to the altar consecrated to the former Caesar and were there sacrificed – three hundred knights and other senators, among them Tiberius Cannutius, who previously during his tribuneship had assembled the populace for Octavian. Of the Perusians and others who were captured there the majority lost their lives, and the city itself, except the temple of Vulcan and the statue of Hera, was entirely destroyed by fire.
>
> Dio 48.14.3–5

There are a number of issues with Dio's account. One is the claim that Octavian ordered a human sacrifice of Roman *equites* and senators at the altar to Julius Caesar. The cult to Julius Caesar in Rome was not inaugurated until sometime in the 20s, which makes the account of a sacrifice of Roman nobles all the more difficult to believe. Appian's version of how Octavian punished the city but saved the members of the Roman elite is easier to accept, not least because with the remark 'and the story is', Dio may be seen to have questioned or at least distanced himself from the version he offers.

On the other hand, there are a number of reasons why Dio's more gruesome account should not be dismissed as out of hand. First, both Suetonius and the philosopher Seneca, who acted as one of Nero's advisors, describe brutal scenes when the city fell (Seneca *Clem.* 11.1, and Suet. *Aug.* 15.1). Suetonius even mentions how other writers had narrated that Octavian selected 300 men among the senators and *equites* and had them sacrificed on the Ides of March. Once again, we find a reference to human sacrifice in relation to the Caesar cult. It seems likely that Dio and Suetonius had read some of the same descriptions of the Battle at Perusia, and Dio is also likely to have read Suetonius. Given that both authors share the same opening that stories were told of how Octavian ordered a sacrifice of Roman nobles, it is reasonable to assume that Octavian was behind a gruesome act of violence after he defeated Lucius Antonius and the opposition in the city. For his part, Appian read about what happened at Perusia in Augustus' autobiography, which of course does not necessarily mean that he is misleading on the battle narrative in general. However, it should be taken into consideration that when he offered his own version of what happened at Perusia, Augustus would want to downplay or ignore an order to sacrifice or execute members of the Roman elite in front of altars.

Appian offers the longest and most detailed account of the battle itself, and the most informative description of the siege and its aftermath. Compared to the distinctly shorter version offered by Dio, Appian provides a detailed picture of the battle. What Dio offers, on the other hand, are glimpses into a different version, one Augustus was not proud of, and one that did not fit the version Dio usually tells about his favourite emperor. It is interesting to note how, just as he did in the case of the proscriptions in 43, Dio makes no effort to explain why Octavian gave the savage order to have Roman nobles cut down at or in the vicinity of some of the city's altars. One explanation might be that he believed it to be true, which again underlines how Dio, whose mission it was to explain and justify Octavian's way to power, wanted to give his readers as accurate an account of the course of the civil war as he could. One of Dio's points is that civil war makes even the most righteous men commit atrocities, something the episode in Perusia helps us to underline. One way to read Dio's coverage of the executions of Perusians and the Roman 'rebels' is to see it as his way of telling his readership how brutal war between citizens was and why it should be avoided at all costs.[7]

Another example where Dio offers a thorough analysis is on the reign of Tiberius. Here the reader is presented with a detailed account of the events that unfolded in 31 CE when the emperor removed from power his trusted prefect Sejanus. Dio describes how the senators were turning their attention towards Sejanus, whom they started to see as the *de facto* ruler of the empire after Tiberius had vacated the city and moved to his villa in Capri. As the emperor becomes aware of Sejanus' improved position in Rome, he feels betrayed and starts planning the fall of Sejanus and at the same time a lesson to the Senate that he is still in full control of the affairs in Rome (Dio 58.9–12).

Dio describes a course of events where Tiberius gives Sejanus and the Senate the impression that Sejanus was to be given tribunician powers, which traditionally would imply that the prefect was intended as Tiberius' partner and perhaps successor. When Sejanus shows up in the Senate, the consul praises him, believing that the prefect was soon to become the emperor's co-ruler. But as he reads out the letter to the rest of the senators it becomes clear that Sejanus is being accused of treason. Under great turmoil, Sejanus is removed from the chamber and executed. Dio offers more than just an account of Sejanus' fall. The description of how the envious and insecure Tiberius staged a scene in the Senate that brought his prefect down and destabilized Rome and the Senate's authority is a story that reveals a lot about the political climate in Rome and how Tiberius was apparently reluctant to come up to Rome and settle the matter himself. When he chose to stay out of Rome, it was because he feared Sejanus and was unsure that he would be able to count on support from the Senate.

Because we lack Tacitus' account of Sejanus' fall, Dio's coverage of the episode is the only detailed description we have of what happened when Tiberius decided to punish his trusted advisor. However, Dio was not only filling a gap left in Tacitus' text. The reader is provided with an analysis of Tiberius' way of operating, and of the motives that the emperor had for bringing Sejanus down in a way that would damage his relationship with the Senate and the consuls. We have no way of knowing what source material Dio used. He may have consulted the acts of the Senate and found Tiberius' letter in the archives, or he may have read Tacitus or other sources who wrote about the episode closer to the event. He may also have had access to sources written by people close to the emperor that are no longer available to us today. In any case, Dio offers a highly valuable account of Tiberius, Sejanus and the political situation in Rome around the time the emperor took down one of his few trusted supporters. This is indispensable to the reconstruction of Roman politics at the time Tiberius tried to run the empire from exile on Capri.

A third example where Dio demonstrates how meticulous a historian he can be may be deduced from his coverage of the reign of Hadrian. The text is not Dio's own but is part of Xiphilinus' excerpts. The reader is offered a multifaceted portrait of this somewhat controversial emperor. Dio's portrait of Hadrian opens with a description of how Hadrian took control of power by staging himself as Trajan's chosen successor, and how his accession was met with opposition. Hadrian, Trajan's nephew, had not been formally adopted or in any other way singled out as the likely successor to the throne but got the support from Trajan's wife who corroborated the story. Dio moves on to describe Hadrian as a hateful and jealous man who removed men of talent, and he details that he was behind the killing of members of the Senate who had questioned his accession to the throne.

On the positive side, Dio emphasized how Hadrian disciplined the army by leading from example and by introducing the soldiers' code of law. A firm hand with the soldiers is something Dio sees as one of the most important qualities in a leader and Hadrian becomes the antithesis of emperors of his own time, Septimius Severus and Caracalla in particular, who tried to buy the support from the armies (Dio 69.94–6). Another of Hadrian's achievements was that he took steps to end what Dio believed were unnecessarily expansive wars (Dio 69.5.1). Again, the contrasts with Trajan and Severus, who both fought wars against Parthia because they wanted the prestige, is noticeable. Another and perhaps more important trait with which Hadrian is credited is how he made necessary arrangements to promote the practice of choosing the new emperor from among the most eligible members of the Senate. Hadrian's own route to power may have been open to question, but by adopting Antoninus Pius and by trying to arrange who Pius was to adopt, Hadrian made every effort to ensure that Rome would not return to dynastic rule in the future.

Judging from what we can retrieve from the excerpts, Dio's readers are provided with a fairly balanced account of an emperor who would have divided people. Hadrian's less attractive characteristics were of a man that Dio would normally think of as unfit to fulfil the role of emperor. However, instead of focusing on the killing of senators or on the other men of talent Hadrian had removed, Dio underlines how the emperor put a stop to the expansive wars and how he tried to change the culture in the army – these come over as more important in the bigger picture than the killing of a few senators or the means by which he came to power. This way of drawing the readers' attention to the stronger and weaker sides of Hadrian offers a more complete picture of an emperor who would have been criticized by many in Rome but also cherished by many Greek men of letters who appreciated his erudition and interest in Greek culture.[8] Also, in this case, the *Roman History* offers a more detailed and nuanced account of what kind of man Hadrian was – he is something other than one who came to power with a palace coup. With his portrait of Hadrian, Dio provides an alternative version to the one that would have circulated in Rome – of how the emperor's nephew falsified his adoption to secure supreme power. Dio also offers a more balanced version than the one told among Greek men of letters that Hadrian was the best emperor Rome had had because of his interests in Greek culture.

Seen as a whole, Dio is best when writing about earlier periods, where he relied on early sources. Compared to his coverage of Roman politics and the reign of the emperors that he experienced first-hand where he relied on his own observations and where his own feelings got in the way, Dio is more analytical and often less self-involved when he worked on earlier periods. Later historians such as Herodian or the author of the *Historia Augusta* would have read the eyewitness reports from Commodus' gladiatorial adventures, the scenes in the Senate where Didius Julianus and Severus threatened the senators, or the report of how Caracalla repeatedly humiliated Dio and his peers on the trip to Asia Minor; they would have found them useful as a source for the political climate in late-second- and early-third-century Rome. However, the portrait of Commodus and the Severan emperors and the coverage of their years in power, is less balanced than the shorter account of Hadrian or the more analytical study of why Tiberius acted in the way he did when he removed Sejanus from power.

To summarize, Dio is at his best when we may disagree with his analyses of Rome's history but also may be inspired by them. His passionate criticism of democracy and free political competition is useful even if it is overstated, just as his praise of monarchical rule is interesting and on a level with later political thinkers such as Machiavelli and Thomas Hobbes, who share many of the same thoughts on absolute rule. Whether Machiavelli read Dio is difficult to determine with any kind of certainty. There are no specific references to *Roman History* in *The Prince*, where many of the same views on enlightened monarchy are available. However, part of Dio's *Roman History* and Xiphilinus' excerpts were available from the fifteenth century, and Niccolò Leoniceno's Latin translation of books 38–60 might have been circulating in parts, even if it was not published until Machiavelli had passed away. Apart from being a refined political thinker, Dio should also be recognized as a universal historian who covered 1,000 years of Roman history in a remarkably coherent fashion. His coverage carries a clear message to the reader of how and why Romans had to protect themselves from the instability and chaos of political freedom. Greed and envy brought Republican Rome to a fall, and even if those failings were contained by monarchy, they continued as a characteristic part of human nature with a potential to flare up if the monarch failed to govern in a stable and enlightened way, in harmony with the Senate and with respect for the mandate on which his powers rested.

Conclusion

As has been discussed in the course of this book, it is a widespread assumption among scholars that when Dio was covering earlier periods of imperial history he was essentially writing the history of his own time; and that his coverage of earlier times was meant as a source of inspiration to the emperor and senators of his own day. Another interpretation of the motives behind Dio's coverage of Rome's political history is that he promoted the senatorial order in order to justify the privileged position of its members, perhaps because in the course of his own lifetime the Senate had come under strong pressure from the army and people in the provincial cities.

If, however, we apply a more holistic approach to the eighty books Dio wrote, the aim of writing the text seems to have been more ambitious than simply to cover as much of Rome's history as possible or to draw up a kind of ideal behaviour that members of the political elite could follow in the future. As we have seen in the course of this book, there are elements in Dio's books that show how he defined the ideal emperor and the ideal form of monarchy, and he included examples of emperors and senators misbehaving. These help the reader to see the difference between competent and incompetent imperial conduct. Book 52 and the dialogue between Maecenas and Agrippa is an example where the ideal emperor and Senate are defined; what Dio describes as a notoriously inadequate Senate in the Late Republic is an example of how one of the political groups came up short.

When read collectively, the *Roman History* comes across as a political history, or more precisely, a history of how Rome's constitution and political culture evolved over time: why Roman politics developed in the way it did, how the changes occurred and the effect they had on the way the Romans organized public affairs, their institutions and political life. Dio's devotion to how Roman politics worked and developed in the *longue durée*, and not just in his own lifetime, is demonstrated throughout his entire work where he discusses the shortcomings of a democratic government and the stability and peace that the right form of monarchy would ensure. He also makes it clear how the wrong kind of monarch was likely to place the entire society under considerable pressure.

The bigger scope with writing the history of Rome's constitutional history is suggested by the paradox in how Dio saw monarchy in its most absolute form as the only viable kind of government for a state the size of Rome, at a moment in time when one problematic emperor after another ruled Rome. This is one of the most important messages in the course of 80 books. Dio's thoughts on monarchical rule, in its most efficient and stable form, and his definitions of what constituted both the ideal and the inadequate emperor respectively, were probably inspired by what he saw when living in Rome, and by his own first-hand experiences with emperors such as Commodus, Septimius Severus, Caracalla and Elagabal. We should recall, however, that there were eccentric emperors with poor or hostile relations with the Senate, particularly in the first century CE, about whom Dio could have read before he encountered Severus and Caracalla. Therefore, there are grounds for believing that Dio's thoughts on monarchy and suitable emperors were not just formed by the conduct of men who came into his life after he had finished collecting material for his books.

When Dio focuses on how the emperor should behave with modesty and should include the senators in the decision-making process, treat them with respect and recognize their elevated position in the society, it is relevant for his own time. However, this concerns the entire imperial period from the reign of Tiberius onwards, and it is a view that Dio shared with most intellectuals across the Empire. The thoughts of how the ideal form of monarchy should be organized is one where the emperors were chosen from among the most qualified men in the state, which in Dio's view were senators with proven military and political records. As Dio demonstrates in book 52, these emperors were still to be given absolute power. In that sense, the other senators were not their equals in the political sense of the word, and they were not intended to have any real power or any right to promote their own political ideas.

In addition, these emperors were to choose their magistrates, officers and new senators, as this was the only way to avoid political chaos and other forms of political competition. It was the emperor's sole responsibility to make sure that new laws were drawn up and implemented. In Dio's vision, the adoptive emperors were also to take advice from their former peers and consider their thoughts and reservations carefully. In this connection, it should be stressed that Dio is not suggesting that the Senate should be given any decisive powers or the opportunity to promote their own candidacy or political programmes.

In Dio's ideal constitution, the right to the throne rests on the willingness to consult the Senate and on how the emperor was selected from among the senatorial elite. Monarchy and the stability it provided in its right form was bigger and more important than political liberty and the freedom to pursue individual ambition; and it was larger than the rule of unqualified emperors because the alternative, a democratic form of government, was considerably worse. Dio never questions the superiority of monarchical rule – not even in the reign of Commodus, Caracalla and Elagabal whom he criticizes for doing a poor job as emperor or for being tyrants. However, instead of discussing alternative solutions, Dio warns against dynastic rule, mostly by emphasizing good examples, such as Nerva's adoption of Trajan, but also in the books he wrote during the reign of Caracalla he maintains that the monarchical reign of the right kind of emperor is the only form of constitution to ensure political stability.

In that sense, Dio's *Roman History* is not just an attempt to cover Rome's political history from foundation to his own time, which in itself was already an ambitious task, but an effort to write a detailed account of how Rome's constitutional set-up changed over the 1,000 years of history he was able to cover. As a man from Bithynia and a second-generation Roman senator who came to Rome in the reign of Marcus Aurelius, Dio was shocked by the accession of Commodus. A period of reasonable stability was followed by decades of political chaos caused by changing emperors and a new period of civil war. Looking back as a man with a profound historic interest, Dio still believed that monarchy was preferable to what he calls democracy.

As we saw in Chapter 1, Dio maintains that democracy was an inferior form of government because political competition between members of the elite and the people's ability to pressurize those in power to promote short-sighted interests failed to offer stability. Only Augustus, or emperors like him who took it upon themselves to lead with modesty and in respect of members of the elite, was able to reduce the threat of civil war. As discussed in Chapter 2, to prove his point Dio offers a series of examples of how, in the age of the republic, Rome was in the hands of a political elite with no real interest in the Commonwealth.

Instead, essentially all members of the Republican political elite did what they felt suited them best to enhance their own wealth, prestige and influence. In addition, the reader is offered a version of Roman history that supports Dio's overall view that Augustus was the man who saved the Romans by introducing his form of absolute rule: it was this type of rule that later emperors often failed to imitate. Dio's preference for monarchical rule and his deployment of highly-selective examples are both a strength and a weakness of his work. In Chapter 1, we discussed how Dio pursued his own hypotheses – that monarchy is the only form of constitution useful for a city the size of Rome – to the point where he misrepresents the episodes and examples he uses. However, Dio is often also the ancient observer who delivers the most thorough account of a specific situation. He is best when he writes about periods that predate his own years in Rome. Here, he has the benefit of earlier sources: archives, letters and the like. This allows him to analyse the information and draw his own conclusions. It is here, in the account of specific episodes – such as the events following the fall of Perusia and the death of Sejanus – Dio may be seen to offer a thorough analysis of a given event. We may disagree with the motives he saw behind the choices that were made, but the analysis is there for us to discuss. Dio is not just covering the course Rome took, he is offering answers to why Roman politics developed as it did.

For those reasons but also because he offers a detailed analysis of Roman politics over more than a millennium, Dio is a more useful source than he is often given credit for, and he should be consulted not just as indispensable evidence for his own lifetime or the age of Augustus, but to Rome's political history more generally. And just as importantly, *Roman History* has much to offer if read in its entirety. It then becomes clear that Dio had a political aim that went beyond the ambition to offer advice to the political elite of his own time. Seen in that light, Dio is analytical in much the same fashion as writers such as Thucydides, Polybius and, for that matter, Sallust. Dio is similarly attentive to how fear, greed and a desire for glory among members of the elite continued to be a destabilizing factor not just in Rome but also in any other state. However, when reading Dio as a source of Rome's political history, we should keep in mind the underlying agenda of how democracy was destined to fail and how Augustus, because he replaced democracy with what Dio saw as a more stable form of constitution, was the one who saved the Romans from their own destruction.

Dio was therefore more aware of the bigger picture in Roman politics than is often acknowledged. He was not simply focusing on his own years or trying to promote the importance of the senatorial order. On the contrary, the *Roman History* may convincingly be read as an attempt to show that an oligarchical elite would always be unable to fulfil the complicated task of governing in a fair and stable fashion. Based on years of experience in Roman politics and a profound historical knowledge, Dio dismisses democracy and questions the sense of political liberty by arguing in favour of monarchy no matter how unfit the emperor turned out to be.

Notes

Introduction

1. Millar 1964, 15; Rich 1990, 1–2.
2. Millar 1964, 17; Rich 1990, 1–2. For the later date of Dio's first consulship see Gabba 1955, 291.
3. Millar 1964, 23–4 and Rich 1990, 3; Potter 2004, 163–4.
4. Scott 2018, 151–2.
5. Potter 2004, 166–7.
6. Bekker-Nielsen 2008, 109–14.
7. Madsen 2009, 90–6.
8. E.g. Woolf 1994, 127–9; Swain 1996, 69–7, on Dio's Greekness see 404–8.
9. Madsen 2009, 91–6.
10. Burde-Strevens 2015, 296–304.
11. Madsen 2009, 124–6.
12. For a recent study of Dio's books 1–21 see Burden-Strevens and Lindholmer 2019.
13. Mallan 2013, 616, 643.
14. Millar 1964, 73.
15. See e.g. Reinhold and Swan 1990, 169–73.
16. On Dio as an accumulator of information see Barrett 2002, 237–8; For how our historian is not in control of the chronology and on his bias in his coverage of the life of Agrippina see Barrett 1996, 203–4.
17. Millar 1964, 179.

Chapter 1

1. Macleod 1979, 58–9; Rees 2011, 79–80. For the way Thucydides' writing influenced numerous historians in antiquity see also Reinhold 1988 22–3, 27, 30–1; Millar 1964, 6; Rich 1990, 11.

2   For a thorough discussion of the political situation in late second century Rome see Potter 2004, 101.
3   Kemezis 2014, 104–12, 115–20.
4   For a similar view on Caesar see Suet. *Caes.* 76–81.
5   Gowing 1992, 35.
6   Reinhold 1988, 165; Adler 2012, 477–8.
7   Madsen 2014.
8   Reinhold 1988, 188–9.
9   Rich 1990, 136–40.
10 Manuwald 1979, 32–9, 280–4.
11 See e.g. Lange 2009, esp. 18–38, 181–8, 198; Rich 2010.
12 Rich 1990, 136.
13 Madsen 2016, 149–51.
14 Fraschetti 2008, 48; Davenport and Mallan 2014, 643–4, 657–8.
15 Madsen 2019, 153.

Chapter 2

1   Lindholmer 2019, 193.
2   Simons 2009, 303–5, 13–14; Kemezis 2014, 104–7.
3   Lindholmer 2019, 195–203.
4   Libourel 1968; Coudry 2019, 154; Lange 2019, 175–6; Lindholmer 2019, 190–1; Madsen 2019, 108–15.
5   Simons 2009, 301, 300–9. Briquel 2016, 136–7; Fromentin 2016, 181, De Franchis 2016, 192, 203–4. On the value of tracing Dio's sources see also Burden-Strevens 2019, 4.
6   Schulz 2019, 312.
7   Madsen 2019, 104–8.
8   Coudry 2019, 141–7.
9   Lange 2019, 178–84.
10 Urso 2016, 13–16.
11 Kemezis 2014, 115–20.
12 Coudry 2016, 38–9, 42–5.
13 Coudry 2016, 35–6; Burden-Strevens 2016, 196–8.

14 Madsen 2016, 144.
15 Madsen 2016, 144–6.
16 For commentary work and translations of Dio Augustan books see Reinhold 1988; Rich 1990; Swan 2004. See also Gowing 1992 for a study of the triumviral period and Manuwald for a combined coverage of the civil war period and the principate. On Dio as a key source on Augustus see Reinhold and Swan 1990.
17 Millar 1964, 46.
18 For a less aggressive Octavian and for an analysis of how the war between Octavian and Antony was not unaviodable see Lange 2009, 50.
19 Talbert 1984, 56–7 and Brunt 1984, 427.

Chapter 3

1 Mecella 2016; Robert 2016.
2 Mecella 2016, 42–8.
3 Robert 2016, 53–9.
4 Millar 1964, 171.
5 Madsen 2016.
6 On how there was no alternative to the political crisis of Late Republican Rome see Christian Meier 1966. See also Meier 1982 for a redefining physiological portrait where Caesar comes across as some who saw the need for changes to the Roman republican constitution but also as one who did not what to set instead of the existing constitutional framework.
7 Lange 2019.
8 Madsen 2014, 31–3.

Bibliography

Adler, E. 'Cassius Dio's Agrippa–Maecenas Debate: An Operational Code Analysis'. *American Journal of Philology* 133, no. 3 (2012): 477–520.

Barnes, T.D. 'The Composition of Cassius Dio's "Roman History"'. *Phoenix* 38, no. 3 (1984): 240–55.

Barrett, A.A. *Agrippina: Sister of Caligula, Wife of Claudius, Mother of Nero.* London and New York: Taylor and Francis, 1996.

—— *Livia: First Lady of Imperial Rome.* New Haven, CT, and London: Yale University Press, 2002.

Bekker-Nielsen, T. *Urban Life and Local Politics in Roman Bithynia.* Aarhus: Aarhus University Press, 2008.

Birquel, D. 'Origines et période royale'. In *Cassius Dion: nouvelles lectures,* V. Fromentin et al. (eds.), 125–41. Bordeaux: Ausonius Éditions, 2016.

Brunt, P.A. 'The Role of the Senate in the Augustan Regime'. *The Classical Quarterly* 34, no. 2 (1984): 423–44.

Burden-Strevens, C.W. 'Ein völlig romanisierter Mann? Identity, Identification, and Integration in the *Roman History* of Cassius Dio and in Arrian'. In *Processes of Cultural Change and Integration in the Roman World,* S. Roselaar (ed.), 287–306. Leiden and Boston: Brill, 2015.

—— 'Fictitious Speeches, Envy, and the Habituation to Authority: Writing the Collapse of the Roman Republic'. In *Cassius Dio: Greek Intellectual and Roman Politician,* C.H. Lange and J.M. Madsen (eds.), 193–216. Leiden and Boston: Brill, 2016.

—— 'Introduction'. In *Cassius Dio's Forgotten History of Early Rome: The Roman History, Books 1–21,* C.W. Burden-Strevens and M.O. Lindholmer (eds), 1–23. Leiden and Boston: Brill, 2019.

Burden-Strevens, C.W. and M.O. Lindholmer (eds.). *Cassius Dio's Forgotten History of Early Rome: The Roman History, Books 1–21.* Leiden and Boston: Brill, 2019.

Cary, E. *Dio Cassius Roman History.* Cambridge, MA: Harvard University Press, 1914–17.

Coudry, M. 'Cassius Dio on Pompey's Extraordinary Commands'. In *Cassius Dio: Greek Intellectual and Roman Politician,* C.H. Lange and J.M. Madsen (eds), 33–50. Leiden and Boston: Brill, 2016.

—— 'The "Great Men" of the Middle Republic in Cassius Dio's *Roman History*'. In *Cassius Dio's Forgotten History of Early Rome: The* Roman History, *Books 1–21,* C.W. Burden-Strevens and M.O. Lindholmer (eds.), 126–64. Leiden and Boston: Brill, 2019.

Davenport, C, and C. Mallan. 'Hadrian's Adoption Speech in Cassius Dio's *Roman History* and the Problems of Imperial Succession'. *American Journal of Philology* 135, no. 4 (2014): 637–68.

Edmondson, J.C. *Dio: The Julio-Claudians. Selections from Books 58–63 of the* Roman History *of Cassius Dio.* London: London Association of Classical Teachers, 1992.

Flower, H.I. *Roman Republics.* Princeton, NJ, and Oxford: Princeton University Press, 2010.

de Franchis, M. 'Tite-Live modèle de Cassius Dion, ou contre-modèle?'. In *Cassius Dion: nouvelles lectures,* V. Fromentin et al. (eds), 191–204. Bordeaux: Ausonius Éditions, 2016.

Fraschetti, A. *Marco Aurelio. La Miseria Della Filosofia.* Rome-Bari: Laterza, 2008.

Fromentin, V. 'Denys d'Halicarnasse, source et modèle de Cassius Dion?'. In *Cassius Dion: nouvelles lectures,* V. Fromentin et al. (eds), 179–90. Bordeaux: Ausonius Éditions, 2016.

Gabba, E. 'Sulla Storia Romana di Cassio Dione'. *Rivista Storica Italiana* 67, (1955): 289–333.

Gowing, A.M. *The Triumviral Narratives of Appian and Cassius Dio.* Ann Arbor: University of Michigan Press, 1992.

Kemezis, A.M. *Greek Narratives of the Roman Empire under the Severans. Cassius Dio, Philostratus and Herodian.* Cambridge: Cambridge University Press, 2014.

Lange, C.H. *Res Publica Constituta: Actium, Apollo and the Accomplishment of the Triumviral Assignment.* Leiden and Boston: Brill, 2009.

—— 'Triumphal Chariots, Emperor Worship and Dio Cassius: Declined Triumphal Honours'. *Analecta Romana Instituti Danici*, 40 and 41 (2016): 21–33.

—— 'Cassius Dio on Violence, Stasis, and Civil War: The Early Years'. In *Cassius Dio's Forgotten History of Early Rome: The Roman History, Books 1–21*, C.W. Burden-Strevens and M.O. Lindholmer (eds), 165–89. Leiden and Boston: Brill, 2019.

—— 'Cassius Dio on Sextus Pompeius and Late Republican Civil War'. In *Cassius Dio and the Late Republic*, J. Osgood and C. Baron (eds). Leiden and Boston: Brill, 2019.

Libourel, J. *Dio Cassius on the Early Roman Republic*. Diss: University of California, 1968.

Lindholmer, M.O. 'Breaking the Idealistic Paradigm: Competition in Dio's Earlier Republic'. In *Cassius Dio's Forgotten History of Early Rome: The Roman History, Books 1–21*, C.W. Burden-Strevens and M.O. Lindholmer (eds), 190–214. Leiden and Boston: Brill, 2019.

Macleod, C.W. 'Thucydides on Faction (3.82–83)'. *Proceedings of the Cambridge Philological Society* 25 (1979): 52–68.

Madsen, J.M. *Eager to be Roman: Greek Response to Roman Rule in Pontus and Bithynia*. London: Duckworth, 2009.

—— 'Patriotism and Ambitions: Intellectual Response to Roman Rule in the High Empire'. In *Roman Rule in Greek and Latin Writing. Double Vision*, J.M. Madsen and R. Rees (eds), 16–38. Leiden and Boston: Brill, 2014.

—— 'Cassius Dio and the Cult of Ivlivs and Roma at Ephesus and Nicaea (51.20.6–8)'. *The Classical Quarterly* 66, no. 1 (2016): 286–97.

—— 'Criticising the Benefactors: The Severans and the Return of Dynastic Rule'. In *Cassius Dio: Greek Intellectual and Roman Politician*, C.H. Lange and J.M. Madsen, 136–158. Leiden and Boston, 2016.

—— 'From Nobles to Villains: The Story of the Republican Senate in Cassius Dio's *Roman History*'. In *Cassius Dio's Forgotten History of Early Rome: The Roman History, Books 1–21*, C.W. Burden-Strevens and M.O. Lindholmer (eds), 99–125. Leiden and Boston: Brill, 2019.

Mallan, C. 'The Style, Method, and Programme of Xiphilinus' Epitome of Cassius Dio's *Roman History*'. *Greek, Roman, and Byzantine Studies* 53 (2013): 610–44.

Manuwald, B. *Cassius Dio und Augustus: Philologische Untersuchungen zu den Büchern 45–56 des Dionischen Geschichtswerkes*. Wiesbaden: Franz Steiner Verlag, 1979.

Mecella, L. 'La ricezione di Cassio Dione alla fine dell'antichità'. In *Cassius Dion: nouvelles lectures,* V. Fromentin et al. (eds), 41–50. Bordeaux: Ausonius Éditions, 2016.

Meier, C. *Res Publica Amissa: Eine Studie zu Verfassung und Geschichte der Späten Römischen Republik.* Wiesbaden: Franz Steiner Verlag, 1966.

—— *Caesar.* Munich: Severin und Siedler, 1982.

Millar, F.G.B. *A Study of Cassius Dio.* Oxford: Clarendon Press, 1964.

Osgood, J. *Caesar's Legacy: Civil War and the Emergence of the Roman Empire.* Cambridge and New York: Cambridge University Press, 2006.

Pelling, C.B.R. 'Biographical History? Cassius Dio on the Early Principate'. In *Portraits: Biographical Representation in the Greek and Latin Literature of the Roman Empire,* M.J. Edwards and S. Swain (eds), 117–44. Oxford: Oxford University Press, 1997.

Potter, D. *The Roman Empire at Bay, AD 180–395.* London: Routledge, 2004.

Rees, W. *Cassius Dio, Human Nature and the Late Roman Republic.* Diss: Oxford, 2011.

Reinhold, M. *From Republic to Principate. An Historical Commentary of Cassius Dio's Roman History Books 49–52 (36–29 BC).* Atlanta, CA: Scholars Press, 1988.

Reinhold, M. and Swan, P.M. 'Cassius Dio's Assessment of Augustus'. In *Between Republic and Empire: Interpretations of Augustus and his Principate,* K. Raaflaub and M. Toher (eds.), 155–73. Berkeley, 1990.

Rich, J.W. *Cassius Dio. The Augustan Settlement (Roman History 53–55.9).* Warminster: Aris and Philips, 1990.

—— 'Deception, Lies, and Economy with the Truth: Augustus and the Establishment of the Principate'. In *Private and Public Lies. The Discourse of Despotism and Deceit in the Graeco-Roman World,* A. Turner et al (eds), 167–91. Leiden and Boston: Brill, 2010.

Roberto, U. 'L'interesse per Cassio Dione in Pietro Patrizio e nella burocrazia palatina dell'età di Giustiniano'. In *Cassius Dion: nouvelles lectures,* V. Fromentin et al. (eds), 51–67. Bordeaux: Ausonius Éditions, 2016.

Schulz, V. 'Defining the Good Ruler: Early Kings as Proto-Imperial Figures in Cassius Dio'. In *Cassius Dio's Forgotten History of Early Rome: The Roman History, Books 1–21,* C.W. Burden-Strevens and M.O. Lindholmer (eds), 311–32. Leiden and Boston: Brill, 2019.

Scott, A. *Emperors and Usurpers: An Historical Commentary on Cassius Dio's* Roman History *Books 79(78)–80(80) (AD 217–229)*. Oxford: Oxford University Press, 2018.

Simons, B. *Cassius Dio und die Römische Republik. Untersuchungen zum Bild des römischen Gemeinwesens in den Büchern 3–35 der* 'Romaika'. Berlin and New York: de Gruyter, 2009.

Steel, C. *The End of the Roman Republic 146 to 44 BC: Conquest and Crisis.* Edinburgh: Edinburgh University Press, 2013.

Swain, S. *Hellenism and Empire: Language, Classicism, and Power in the Greek World AD 50–250.* Oxford: Oxford University Press, Clarendon, 1996.

Swan, P.M. *The Augustan Succession: An Historical Commentary on Cassius Dio's* Roman History *Books 55–56 (9 BC–AD 14)*. Oxford: Oxford University Press, 2004.

Talbert, R. 'Augustus and the Senate'. *Greece and Rome* 31.1 (1984): 55–63.

Urso, G. 'Cassius Dio's Sulla: Exemplum of Cruelty and Republican Dictator'. In *Cassius Dio: Greek Intellectual and Roman Politician,* C.H. Lange and J.M. Madsen, 13–32. Leiden and Boston: Brill, 2016.

Woolf, G. 'Becoming Roman, Staying Greek: Cultural Identity and the Civilizing Process in the Roman East'. *Proceedings of the Cambridge Philological Society* 40 (1994): 116–43.

Index

Actium 102
Afranius, L. 78
Africa 1, 6, 40, 94
Agrippa 14, 17, 27, 38, 86, 115
Albinus, D. Septimius, emperor (197) 19–20, 22, 26, 28, 91, 94, 77, 99, 101
Alexander Severus (222–235) 2, 6, 14, 55, 93
Alexandria 11, 35, 102
Ancus Marcius 62
Antioch 11
Antoninus Pius, emperor (138–161) 54, 112
Antonius, L. 107–9
Antony, Mark 16, 32–3, 37, 43, 45, 59, 83, 86, 102, 105, 107
Appian 3, 34, 59, 68, 70, 84, 108–9
Apronianus, P. Pedo 98
Aristides 7, 40
Aristotle 30, 31
Armenia 76, 86
Asia Minor 1, 3–4, 70, 73, 75–6, 104, 113
Asia, the province 5, 70, 98, 104
Athens 11, 71
Augustus/Octavian 9, 14–17, 22–3, 27–8, 32–3, 36–8, 39, 40–8, 55, 59, 73, 82–9, 95, 97, 99, 101–10, 118–19

Baebius Marcellinus 98
Barea Soranus 3
Bibulus, M. 80–1
Bithynia 1, 3–4, 75, 93, 104, 118
Britannia 26
Britannicus 89
Brundisium 77
Brutus, M. Junius 107
Byzantium 20

Caligula, emperor (37–41) 9, 26, 51, 55, 60, 89, 91
Camillus, M. Furius 64–5
Campania 2, 93
Cannutius, T. 108
Cappadocia 76
Capri 110–11
Caracalla, emperor (209–217) 1–2, 6, 14–15, 19, 26, 48, 55, 60, 91, 93–4, 97, 112–13, 116–17
Carthage 21, 31, 34, 64
Cassius Apronianus 3
Cassius Asclepiodotus 3–4
Cassius Chrestus 4–6
Cassius Longinus, G. 107
Cassius Philiscus 3–4
Cato the Younger 67, 107
Cicero, Marcus Tullius 8, 11, 15, 33, 76
Cilicia 3, 8, 75
Cinna, L. Cornelius 71
Claudius, emperor (41–54) 9–10, 40, 89–90
Cleopatra 59, 86
Commodus, emperor (180–192) 1, 8, 14, 19, 25–6, 48, 51, 53, 91, 97, 113, 116–17
Constantinople 95–6
Corcyra 71
Crassus, M. Licinius 75, 79, 80

Dalmatia 1, 6, 8, 94
Delphi 65
Didius Julianus, emperor (193) 14, 19, 25, 92, 97
Dionysius of Halicarnassus 59, 61
Domitian, emperor (81–96) 55, 60, 89

Egypt 35, 86, 102 103–4

Elagabal, emperor (218–222) 1, 15, 55, 97, 116–17
Ephesus 11, 103–4

Fabius Maximus, Q. 65
Falerii 65
Fulvia 107

Gabinius, Aulus 73–5
Galatia 78
Galba, emperor (68) 3
Germania 52
Germanicus 89
Gracchus, Tiberius 9, 16, 34–6, 59, 66, 68–9, 73

Hadrian, emperor (117–138) 7, 17–18, 51, 53, 91, 111–13
Hannibal 65
Herodian 23, 94, 98, 113

Italy 34, 36, 40, 49, 68, 72, 77–8, 80, 104, 107

John the Lydian 94–6
Julia Domna 6, 60
Julius Caesar, G. 9, 15–16, 20, 29, 32–3, 36–7, 43–5, 67, 73, 76, 78–85, 87–9, 102, 103–4, 107–8
Justinian, emperor (527–565) 94, 96

Lepidus 32, 37, 43, 86
Livy 11, 59, 61, 63
Lucullus, L. Licinius 75–8

Machiavelli 113–14
Macrinus, emperor (217–218) 1, 15, 19
Maecenas 14, 17, 27, 38–9, 42, 49, 51, 85, 115
Manilius, Gaius 75
Marcus Aurelius, emperor (161–180) 2, 4, 7, 12, 18, 50, 51, 53–4, 97, 100, 118

Marius, Gaius 9, 70–1, 97
Metellus Celer, Q. Caecilius 78
Mithridates 46, 70–3, 75–7

Naulochus 86
Nero, emperor (54–68) 3, 28, 51, 55, 89, 91, 109
Nerva, emperor (96–98) 40, 50–3, 90, 117
Nicaea 3–6, 20, 93, 100, 103–4
Niccolò Leoniceno 114
Nicomedia 1, 4, 104
Niger, G. Pescennius, emperor (193–194) 19, 20, 25–6, 28, 92, 94, 99
Numa 61, 64

Octavianus M. 35

Pannonia 2, 6, 94
Parthia 86, 107, 112
Pergamum 1, 6, 103–4
Pertinax, emperor (193) 1, 18–19, 25, 92, 97
Perusia (modern Perugia) 23, 45–6, 84, 86, 107–10, 119
Peter the Patrician 94, 96
Pharsalus 81, 84
Philippi 107
Philostratus 7
Plancius Varus 4–5
Plato 30
Pliny the Younger 50, 94–5
Plotina 53
Plutarch 68
Polybius 13, 30, 119
Pompeius, Sextus 86, 105, 107
Pompey the Great 9, 16, 29, 46, 67, 73–83, 85, 87, 102
Pontus 70–1, 76

Quintilian 8

Romulus 61–2, 95
Rufus, M. Minucius 65

Sallust 11, 34, 95, 119
Sejanus 23, 110–11, 113, 119
Seneca 109
Septimius Severus, emperor (193–211) 1, 6, 12, 19–20, 22, 25–6, 48, 91–4, 96–9, 101–2, 112–13, 116
Servius Tullius 62–4
Sicily 86
Smyrna 1, 6, 11
Spain 40, 78
Suetonius 46–7, 86, 89, 109
Sulla, Cornelius 9, 29, 70–3, 77, 97
Sulpicius Rufus, P. 70
Syria 25, 94

Tacitus 3, 11, 34–5, 46, 50, 89, 95, 105, 111
Tarquinius Priscus 62–4

Tarquinius Superbus 31, 62–3
Thomas Hobbes 113
Thucydides 7, 11, 23, 25, 71, 119
Tiberius, emperor (14–37) 23, 89, 90, 110–11, 113, 116
Tigranes 75–6
Titus, emperor (79–81) 60
Trajan, Emperor (98–117) 18, 50–3, 90–1, 94, 111–12, 117
Tullia 63

Veii 64–5
Velleius Patercullus 34–5, 59, 95
Vespasian, emperor (69–79) 51, 55, 90–1
Vitellius, Emperor (69) 91

Xiphilinus 9–10, 18, 93, 96, 100, 111, 114

Lightning Source UK Ltd.
Milton Keynes UK
UKHW010815080223
416661UK00011B/470